THE EXAM SECRET

In the same series

Brush Up Your Grammar
The Right Way To Spell
General & Social Letter Writing

All uniform with this book

Where to find *Right Way*

Elliot *Right Way* take pride in our editorial quality, accuracy and value-for-money. Booksellers everywhere can rapidly obtain any *Right Way* book for you. If you have been particularly pleased with any one title, do please mention this to your bookseller as personal recommendation helps us enormously.

Please send to the address on the back of the title page opposite, a stamped, self-addressed envelope if you would like a copy of our *free catalogue*. Alternatively, you may wish to browse through our extensive range of informative titles arranged by subject on the Internet at **www.right-way.co.uk**

We welcome views and suggestions from readers as well as from prospective authors; do please write to us or e-mail:
info@right-way.co.uk

THE EXAM SECRET

HOW TO MAKE THE GRADE

Barbara Brown

RIGHT WAY

Set in 11½pt Times by County Typesetters, Margate, Kent.
Printed and bound in Great Britain by Cox & Wyman Ltd., Reading, Berkshire.

The *Right Way* series is published by Elliot Right Way Books, Brighton Road, Lower Kingswood, Tadworth, Surrey, KT20 6TD, U.K. For information about our company and the other books we publish, visit our web site at www.right-way.co.uk

CONTENTS

PREFACE

This book has been written to try to answer some of the questions asked by many students over many years and, in doing so, to provide practical solutions to perceived problems. It is very much hoped that the book will give confidence as well as useful advice to those who read it.

Students at all levels are uncertain, confused and worried at times. This book attempts to change an attitude of 'Can't' to 'Can do!'

Having said that, it is not intended to suggest that all study is painful and problematic. The reverse is the case. Studying and learning should be a most enjoyable and exciting experience at whatever age we begin. The book intends to show you, as a student, how to make best use of your time and potential and how to enjoy your course and succeed in your final examinations.

It may seem that the book ranges rather widely at times from basic to advanced work. Yes it does, intentionally so. Students are advised to 'keep it simple' and yet are also expected to deal with some complex vocabulary and sentence structure as a matter of course.

There is no apology for including 'basic' language work or 'basic' reference of any kind. A lack of such knowledge can handicap even advanced students who may feel that, although they *don't* know, they *should* know and cannot possibly ask!

Introduction to an extensive vocabulary is of use to all and no harm is done by having to "look it up".

We all begin our studies with some idea in mind of where we wish to go, what we wish to do, what we are studying 'for'. The journey is not easy, but dreaming about what we *could* do or *might* do will not get us to the end of the journey or even to the beginning.

Think of the saying "a journey of a thousand miles starts with a single step". And so it does. Without that step there is no journey and, therefore, no arrival. Think of this when studying becomes hard, when it is tempting to give up or to give in.

Do not give up. Look for solutions to your problems or difficulties. Think of them as 'temporary'. Solutions *will* be there. Some of them are in this book!

1

ORGANISING STUDY TIME

When planning the organisation of your own learning you need to have a realistic understanding of your own life style. By this is meant an understanding of the demands made by other people and circumstances upon you, and also your own willingness to make demands upon yourself. Some aspects of our lives are of course more difficult to control than others. This chapter will suggest ways in which individual students can begin to think positively about establishing maximum control over their own particular organisational and time problems. Be aware also that we are not just minds; we are bodies too. We are complex, emotional beings. All these things affect our ability to study and to learn.

There are two clear areas which must be considered when organising ourselves to study. Firstly, the formal demands of school, college or university, and secondly, the informal demands of other areas of our lives.

Formal demands on our time

Formal demands include a requirement to attend a lecture or lessons, practical work sessions, tutorials and field trips and to be at particular places at specified times. Other formal requirements are the completion of set tasks, essays, assignments and dissertations to deadlines set by our teachers or tutors. In between all these activities are others which must take place in order for the first to happen at all.

Remember travel time. If you do not live on campus or near to your school, college or university, then you must allocate time to travel. Do try to organise journeys to include not just attendance at formal lectures or lessons, but to collect material, visit the library, deliver and collect work, use computers, see people, make appointments, arrange sports fixtures perhaps and maybe your social life as well. Make lists of what you need to do. Plan it. Economising on travel time can save money too.

Have a planner for your year's study. On it mark the requirements that you know of term by term. Often students are given an outline plan of what is expected of them for the year. Note what you know for certain immediately, adding information as you are given more. Find out from each teacher or tutor, if possible, what they plan for you in terms of essays and assignments. Note how many you will be expected to do and how long you will be allowed to complete them. Naturally you will have carefully entered the beginnings and endings of terms and half-terms, if you know them already. These dates will have given you the basic structure on which to work.

When you have completed the entries on your planner as far as you can, you will then be able to see at a glance exactly what your time-scales will be. If, for example, your planner shows that you have a field trip of some kind arranged towards the end of the second term, then any work due in by the end of that term needs to be completed before you go. Other than the field trip, work of course! It is obvious really, but experience has taught that the temptation to leave work until the last minute is universal among students. The belief that it will 'only take a day or two' is normally quite mistaken. Often, it is only when an assignment is begun that you realise how much is involved and that all the books needed are on loan already. Panic ensues, unnecessarily. Please do not make the mistake of thinking that you can complete work whilst actually on a field trip. It is very doubtful that you will do this. There will be other things for you to do. That is why you are there!

So, complete your planner as far as you can. Fill in with other requirements as and when they occur. If, for example, you are told the dates of examinations, then you will need to plan the time to begin your revision. You will now have a good idea of how to spend your time and energy over the next few weeks or months.

The next thing to do is to complete a weekly timetable which will show exactly how your days are to be filled with attendance at school or college. How much 'free' time will you have? Will there be sufficient time for you to travel home between classes or will it be more economical with time, energy and money to work on campus in that 'free' time? Make sure you understand your timetable. This may seem an unnecessary piece of advice but much time can be wasted by arriving at lectures or lessons which do not exist, and not arriving at those that do.

Apart from wasting your own time if you miss appointments in this way, you waste the time of others.

However, let us suppose that you have organised yourself perfectly so far. You have clearly written plans for your study and attendances. You know what is expected of your time. What are you going to do with it?

Practical study
Your previous planning will have decided 'when' you study. Now you want to decide 'where'. Is it convenient for you to work at home, or are you lucky enough to have a study room of your own on campus? Would you prefer to work on campus, in the library or in a communal study room? Sometimes

you will need to do that anyway if your work requires access to materials or technology that cannot be borrowed or removed, or if you need to work with others.

As the chapter on learning shows, ideally you need peace and comfort for study. This is not always easy to achieve and it does not mean relaxing in an armchair! What you do need is a quiet space, preferably a room in which you can be alone, without the distractions of TV, radio, children playing, babies crying, or other people and their activities. Then you need a table or desk which is large enough to take your work and materials, neatly arranged, and which is perfectly stable. A wobble can be so very irritating when you are trying to concentrate. Also, you will do best with a chair on which you can be really comfortable whilst working, writing or reading. Not an armchair, but an upright chair with a back rest which gives you the support you need to sit straight for some time and which is the correct height for you to work at your desk.

Nearby, and within easy reach, you will want to have your books and other references. Make sure that paper, folders, pens, pencils, rubbers, rulers and mathematical instruments, calculator, dictionary, thesaurus and anything else that you may use are readily available. If you have to keep getting up and wandering about to find things you need to use, you will soon lose concentration, become irritated and less interested in what you are doing. From there it is a short step to stopping studying 'just for today', until tomorrow when of course you may do the same thing again.

Lack of organisation of the workplace is a perfect recipe for procrastination, especially when there is something else to do which appeals more strongly. At times we have to make ourselves work even when we don't feel at all work-inclined. The only way to deal with this feeling is to begin working. Once you begin it becomes easier to continue and you can become involved more in what you are doing.

Keep a timer, clock or watch to hand. Plan yourself a set time for study, say two or three hours, whenever is convenient within your day. Allow yourself a short break after approximately one hour. The time spent studying differs with individuals but a break helps most people. Make sure, however, that you restart your study (and your timer) after the break. More will be said about the use of time control in the chapter on examination preparation. Working like this now will provide you with practice.

In your break, reward yourself. Have a sandwich (you could prepare this beforehand to have it waiting for you), snack, coffee or something you enjoy and which will boost your energy levels. Study is tiring, so stand, stretch, yawn, and wriggle your shoulders to your ears. You will possibly ache from sitting, writing and concentrating. Promise yourself a treat when you have completed your intended study time to your own satisfaction. Be nice to yourself. You have worked hard.

When you work is up to you. Some students work best late in the day. Others perform better earlier. Formal and informal commitments will determine the time available to you to a large extent. When you sit down to work, decide how much time you will allocate to each task or subject. Use your timer to control your decision. Be realistic about the division of time and how much you can do in one session. Arrange a weekly work timetable if possible. Use your planner. You cannot write a creative essay and write up field trip notes in the same work session; certainly you cannot if either is to be of an acceptable standard.

Some people suggest that it is best to begin work with a subject or topic that you enjoy and then turn to the less preferred work later. This depends on whether you are the kind of person who prefers to eat the crust or the pie first! If you begin with the favoured work it may then be difficult to leave that topic for one which is less appealing, whereas, if the disliked work is done first, you may become so engrossed in what you are doing that you are reluctant to leave it. Your friendly timer will release you at the planned time anyway and you will be able transfer your attentions to the other work with a clear conscience, a sigh of relief and the satisfaction of having done your duty!

Whatever way you choose, the less preferred work has to be done. If you are the conscientious student that you must be, having read this far, you will know that there is always a good feeling of satisfaction when self-discipline asserts itself over preference!

Informal demands
Informal demands include family and domestic arrangements, paid work, outside study, eating and sleeping time. Important too are recreation, sports maybe, hobbies and friends!

Much of the above we cannot avoid or would not wish to avoid. We must respond to physical needs. We must sleep and eat. No one works best when tired and hungry, however determined they may be. People do differ, of course, as we do not all need exactly the same amount of food, sleep or play. It is important though that each student understands his or her own needs and is aware of personal limitations. If you really cannot function without 8 hours sleep, then 8 hours you must have whenever possible. Never mind that your friend appears to be bursting with energy after a series of all-night parties, *you* cannot do this.

Look after yourself. Missing meals makes you tired, affects your ability to think and makes you cross. You may not realise this but it is very true. Your body is an engine that needs fuel. A car cannot run without petrol: you cannot function without food. Try to eat wisely and at sensible times. It is often not appreciated how much energy we use when we study. However tight finances may be, do not economise on meals.

There are only so many hours in a day and, however hard we try, we cannot stretch them. However, we can try to spend those hours as efficiently and economically as possible. All students do not have the same amount of study time. A lucky student may be able to concentrate solely on his studies, without financial worries or concerns over the extraneous demands on his time. Many of us have to juggle academic work with other aspects of our lives. This is particularly the case with mature students who have families to care and provide for, with or without a partner. It is also quite often the case that younger students are expected to take a large share of responsibility for brothers and sisters and household duties. They are still expected to work towards their own achievements when they can. Such demands make student life more difficult, but not necessarily impossible.

For students with the above responsibilities, what exactly are the jobs which need to be done? Can they be organised, as is study time, to make the best possible use of time and energy? Remember that energy expenditure is important too. Save as much of this as you can. Spend your energy allocation with care!

Perhaps it is possible for you to plan meals well ahead with the week's menus for each day written down. Can much of the food preparation be done ahead so that time spent in this way during the week is minimised? If you have basic meals prepared and extras such as vegetables cleaned and ready, it takes only minutes to cook and serve. Such planning and preparation will also make it possible to give the menu list to someone else and point them in the direction of the fridge, microwave or oven. There are probably many other tasks which are expected of you: taking children to and from school, playgroup or nursery, the daily care of small children, washing, cleaning, spending important time with them – can you share these journeys with someone else?

It is not always children who are demanding of our time. Within families, parents and grandparents can be reliant upon us too. Reconciling our different roles, our own needs, and the needs of others, is not easy.

It is of great help if other family members understand how important your study is to you and how important your study is potentially to them. If they will support you in any of the areas mentioned by doing what they can to help you, giving encouragement and caring about your success, you are very lucky indeed. Remember, your successes and achievements can benefit your family as well as yourself. For example, research does show that children, particularly boys, with an educated mother are more likely to do well at school. That is only one advantage. There are many others including, of course, the possibility of improved finances. These are good ideas to hold on to when life becomes hard.

Today, many students find (as some always have!) that they need to supplement any grant-based income by paid work in term time as well as during the vacations. Thorough organisation of their time is absolutely vital for such students. Those of you who must work at this pace need to be very determined and maybe even rather selfish in the use of your time. Sometimes it is possible in such cases for the attainment of qualifications to be spread over a longer period of time to give more breathing space. Doing this will not devalue the worth of your final achievement.

Mature students and those of you with responsibilities as carers should make sure that your school, college or university knows about and understands your situation. Don't struggle on alone. You may have been allocated a 'personal' tutor, in which case you can go to that person and discuss your problems with him. On the other hand, you may find that you can talk more easily to another member of staff. Arrange to discuss matters with that person instead. It may be that arrangements can be made to make life easier for you: perhaps some attendances are not as important as others and you can be excused or perhaps some timetabling can be re-arranged or adjusted to your advantage. Difficult circumstances are, of course, not an excuse to avoid work and responsibility, but it does make sense to find out if these can be alleviated in some way. There may even be a possibility of financial help, particularly with work materials and books. If your circumstances are not known to those in authority, they cannot help you.

Recreation

'How,' you may ask, 'in the light of all that has been said so far, will I even be able to find time for recreation?'

You will and you should. Remember the rewards and treats you are to give yourself after completing your time-tabled work? Time spent on recreation is not wasted time.

Exercise, especially outdoor exercise, helps not just the body but the mind and emotions as well. The body will be more relaxed, and consequently will feel better, the mind will be more refreshed and more alert, and emotions will have a chance to unwind, thereby releasing tension.

Try to maintain at least some of your hobbies or use the facilities of your school or college to develop new ones. Involve yourself in music, dance, creative arts, cooking, riding, walking, sports of all kinds – anything which you find you enjoy. Now is the time to do things you had not thought of before, to take part in activities that had perhaps seemed improbable. A new world of experience could be open to you.

There will be times of course, during your student life, when you will need stern discipline to deny yourself such enjoyable activities, but only temporarily. It will be worth it, as worries about work not done, lack of examination preparation and overdue essays would spoil your enjoyment anyway. The pleasures of recreation are so much greater with a clear mind and, most importantly, a feeling of self-respect.

Our friendships are important too. We all need to be able to share our worries, ideas, understandings and pleasures with others. Time spent with friends, sharing work as well as play, is particularly helpful when we are under pressure. Pressure can be nice as well as nasty, please note! However, the pressure you put on yourself by neglecting your own work requirements will negate the advantages of an afternoon spent sunbathing and chatting, as you will then have to spend an evening frantically scribbling and trying to 'read' several books at once.

If your friends cannot understand this then they are not your friends. Let them spend the sunny afternoon as they wish. They are not your responsibility. You are.

To sum up
1.   Be realistic about yourself and your life-style. What can you honestly expect of yourself in your particular circumstances?
2.   Plan the formal demands on your time. Use:
(a) A yearly planner (macro-planning)
(b) A weekly planner (micro-planning)
(c) A daily planner (timetable – very micro!)
3.   Maximise the use of essential travel time.
4.   Become aware of your timescale.
5.   Be aware of 'free' time and relate this to informal time demands, e.g. visits to the dentist and so on.
6.   Do not procrastinate (put things off).
7.   Be practical. Be clear about the when, where and how, of your study.

8. Organise the physical aspects of study (chairs, desk, materials etc.)
9. Time yourself.
10. Treat yourself.
11. Look after yourself (Eat! Sleep! Play!).
12. Respect yourself.
13. Look to the future when life is hard.
14. Ask, if you need help.

Realise that flexibility is only possible if your study is firmly structured. You will need some leeway. Paradoxically, structure is the only way to 'free' your time.

2

LEARNING AND REMEMBERING

Little pitchers?

Student teachers are frequently told that children should not be seen as little pots to be filled (with information) but as candles to be lit (with the flame of learning); a poetic affirmation of the belief that the job of a teacher is to initiate a love of learning in his pupils and also to provide the means by which his pupils can learn. This is a very attractive sentiment and certainly true to the extent that the development of a love for learning makes the labour of study much easier. It becomes a labour of love in fact, or possibly not even a 'labour' but a delight.

It is true that children want to learn, it is human to want to learn, to find out, to understand, to be able to do something for oneself. Yes indeed, children (and all small animals!) learn through play. We must seriously ask though, what do they learn? Structured, formal learning involves effort, on the part of the teacher and also of the pupil or student.

Many would-be students claim that they cannot learn because they cannot 'remember'. The ability to learn and the ability to recall are confused here. If you cannot 'remember', how is it that you are reading this? How did you get so far? Stop for one moment and consider how well your memory serves you in life, how many things you take for granted that you can do, even without thinking about them!

A person (or any animal!) who has learnt something, anything, changes his behaviour. He is now able to do something he has not been able to do before. He has added to his repertoire of what he can do and understand and is poised to develop further. Think of the immense amount of physical, mental, emotional and behavioural learning that children experience throughout the short years of their childhood. Think then what you yourself can do now, superimposed upon this early, incredible learning achievement. The obvious of course: walking, running, dancing, swimming, using knife and fork and spoon. The more advanced skills requiring the development of greater hand, eye and brain co-ordination: reading, writing and arithmetic. Can you draw, paint, ride a bike, drive a car, do embroidery, play the piano, read music, and operate a computer? How talented we are.

It was once said that a teacher cannot be taught to teach. Nonsense, of course they can. Not only does a teacher need to learn the subject or subjects they intend to teach, they must also learn how to teach it and, most importantly, how to teach their pupils how to learn. This chapter intends to do exactly that, to teach you how to teach yourself to learn and, on the way to that goal, to ensure you develop the confidence and techniques which will help you, as an individual, to recall what you have learned.

Walk before you run
A child wants to crawl, to stand, to walk and then tries to run. After many determined attempts, most children achieve their first wobbly stagger with great triumph. It is an achievement. The saying 'Do not try to run before you can walk' applies very much also to all learning. It is not

possible to cope with advanced study until the basics have been mastered. It is not possible to cope with trigonometry or algebra for example unless the basic arithmetical concepts have been understood and learned. You may be a genius, of course, in which case you have probably understood a great deal without consciously registering that you have done so. Most of us are not like that.

Many 'failures' to learn result simply from the lack of previous knowledge. Students are sometimes unaware of what they do not know. If this sounds silly, it isn't. If you do not know then you are not conscious of a gap in your knowledge. How could you be? This situation can arise very easily through a short period of illness, an absence, then missed work, a vital piece of understanding forever missing, or a misunderstanding not corrected.

Sometimes a teacher, brilliant in regard to the subject he teaches, is quite unable to appreciate the failure of a student or pupil to grasp a wider concept, not realising that the very simple connections and perceptions which the teacher takes for granted have not been made clear. This student in many instances considers the failure to understand, to work correctly, to *remember*, to be his own *fault*. He feels he cannot *learn* this subject and feels 'stupid'. Such students also often, quite mistakenly, assume that everyone else in the group has no problem at all. Really?

If you are in this situation, it is sensible at this point to consider whether you have heard correctly. Can you hear the teacher? Can you see the visual aids used? Is the teacher's voice clear? Have you heard the page reference correctly?

Sadly, in a genuine wish to inspire rather than stultify their charges, some teachers in recent years have placed emphasis on 'learning by doing', interpreted as finding out by trial and error for many small children at school. Maybe this has happened to some of you? If it has, take heart.

There is undoubtedly some knowledge which needs to be

taught and learned. I am thinking of basic educational information here: being taught how to write, the sound and name
of letters and their differences, arithmetic, multiplication
tables, spelling and the terminology for different subject
areas. No teacher of sport would expect their pupils to play
a football match (or any other match) against an opposing
side without first teaching the rules, providing practice time
and insisting on discipline in order to do so. Why should
academic work be any different? No pupil can be expected
to learn without being shown how, when and where, and
being given the opportunity to practise what they have
learnt, not just once, but several times.

Active learning

Learning is not achieved by osmosis (look this up if you do
not know what it means). Learning is an active process.
Successful learning depends on student involvement in what
is happening. Feedback is important. Did it work, do you
understand? Was your work correct? If not, why not? Your
teachers or tutors should tell you by marking your work,
making constructive comments about what you have done,
suggesting what you could have done, encouraging and
helping you. Do not be afraid of making mistakes. We all
make mistakes and they can teach us a great deal, as long as
we know what they are.

However expert and knowledgeable your teacher may be,
you will not learn unless you become actively involved in
your learning. It is important that your teacher is aware of
any difficulties you may have. A well-remembered student
of mine once said 'What you don't realise, Miss, is that
although reading all those pages of homework is easy for
you, for me it is like climbing five flights of stairs!' She was
a good student and one who succeeded in her ambitions
through hard work and determination. I was an ashamed

teacher who had been unaware until then of the existence of such a problem and of the tremendous pressure on the student.

Conversely, there are students who seem to think that knowledge can be acquired with little or no effort on their part. They seem to think that it can be 'caught' like a virus, like 'flu. Unfortunately, this does not happen. Turning up for lessons or lectures, gazing at the teacher, opening a book and staring at it whilst thinking of something else, gets no learning done. We learn by using our eyes, ears and minds, by encouraging our brains, noting, querying, asking, investigating and experiencing. We do all this quite naturally and unconsciously throughout our normal lives. When engaged in formal learning, we must do those things deliberately and consciously.

Some learning theory

Psychology offers two learning theories, often considered to be mutually exclusive. As theories, yes, perhaps they are; they are very different ways of thinking. However, for educational purposes they are both valid.

First, there is Behavioural Psychology. This approach emphasises learning as the result (or outcome) of a response to experience, pleasant or unpleasant. It originates from work done by the Russian Behavioural Scientist, Pavlov, whose experiments with dogs led to the terminology we are using.

Pavlovian theory refers to 'conditioned reflexes', which is where a response to a situation is automatically triggered by the association which one's mind makes with that situation, based on past experience. That is to say that, if your mind remembers good things about a situation, your response will be a favourable one; if you remember bad things about it, you will feel uncomfortable. The theory sees behavioural change as the result of rewarding or unrewarding experiences. This is basic learning which is common to all living things and is widely used today in dog training for example. (Ask yourself why the dog always barks at the postman? The postman goes away after his attack on the front door. Very rewarding!) We can all think of experiences which we would either wish to repeat or avoid repeating. Such learning depends on feedback to become part of our changed behaviour.

Another theoretical approach is Gestält theory. When we say 'The whole is greater than the sum of its parts', we are referring to this way of thinking, which emphasises the importance of learning with understanding rather than through automatic response. Consider, how could you apply this idea to an organism? How much does the physical description of a human being describe you, your best friend, or member of your family? How much does a music score tell you about the emotions the music can create in a listener?

These approaches to learning can also be related to others you may have heard about. Study books refer to 'serialist' or 'linear' as opposed to 'holistic' learning. All this means is that learning which is based on understanding is more dependable than that which is not. Understanding is our goal, but how do we get there?

Ask yourself how can you understand anything if you have no knowledge of it? How can you learn to read, write and pronounce words if you have not learnt the names of the letters of the alphabet and the sounds those letters make? How can you 'understand' decimals if you do not know they operate by using the concept of ten? How can you possibly understand fractions if you have not been taught that the denominator denotes the division of the whole into *equal* parts?

Learning is not a guessing game

The hoped for and intended result of learning is understanding. Understanding, however, is the final outcome of lots of smaller 'understandings' which must originate from the gradual accumulation of knowledge. There are also many things which we 'know' which we might confess we do not 'understand'. To think about it, we can never have a 'final' outcome of learning and understanding because, hopefully, we never do stop learning. How boring life would be if we did.

Aids to learning

Today we have access to learning aids at which previous generations would marvel. At the simplest level we have calculators and, at the most advanced, complex computer systems which will seemingly do our work for us. Actually, they won't. No calculator is completely reliable, no system is infallible, just as no ruler or tape is an absolutely correct measure.

These aids need to be seen as the servants they are, and should be, if they are to be used to help us to work at greater speed and efficiency. No mechanical system can replace the human brain in its capacity to learn. It is said that no human being has ever experienced the use of his brain to its full capacity. We only ever use a small part of its potential. Some people develop more of their mental abilities than others maybe, but never as much as they could. It is also said that, because of our brains, we can take our personal computer systems and calculators with us wherever we go. However, if our brain does not contain very much then it will not be of very much use. Hence learning!

If you have mathematical knowledge you will know if your calculator gives the wrong answer and you will be able to deal with the problem yourself – hopefully. If you do not have the knowledge you are lost.

If you do not know your subject very well and rely on a computer to give you information which you do not understand, you will probably use the information incorrectly, your work will not make sense and you will have learned nothing.

Learning techniques

Different people learn differently. Just as we have different likes, dislikes and abilities, so too do we respond differently to different learning techniques. Find out which technique is the best for you. Probably your best approach will be a combination of methods. You need to develop a conscious awareness of how you learn. Remember what has been said about sight and hearing. We need to maximise the use of all our faculties to learn. Be honest with yourself if you have problems. A difficulty faced honestly can usually be overcome. Many successful students have experienced problems with their sight and hearing and have won through in spite of being disadvantaged. Be encouraged.

Some of us learn just by listening and talking. We are responsive to 'aural' cues. Others prefer to look, see, watch and read to make mental and written notes. Some have what is called a 'photographic' memory where they can remember the page number and the place on the page of what they want to recall; they can 'see' it in their 'mind's eye'. Very useful. We cannot all do this unfortunately.

Research suggests that there are 3 kinds of student.

1. The Cue Seekers

Cue Seekers actively elicit information. They ask, query, respond, and involve themselves. They see their situation as a 'problem' and look for ways (strategies) to deal with it. 'Please Sir?'

2. The Cue-conscious

The cue-conscious student is able to pick up hints and can make associations for himself from what he hears and sees. 'Ah! So that's it!' This does of course imply concentration and attention.

3. The Cue-deaf

Teachers despair! Cue-deaf students do not respond to information heard or seen. Their minds are not attuned to what is happening around them. Before we condemn, let us think once more about possible reasons. Avoidance or embarrassment? Can the student hear? Can they see the board?

A good way to learn is to teach. Perhaps you find that you can work well with others. In group work, ideas and understandings can be shared and expanded to the advantage of all involved. Explaining to others is always helpful, as you need to understand before you explain. Seminars may give you the opportunity to 'teach' and discuss in this way, particularly if you are expected to answer questions. In order to give a seminar to fellow students you will need to do a lot of background work beforehand. Failing an audience, it does help to talk to yourself! Honestly! Be your own audience. You could tape yourself, then listen, then 'argue' and question.

Does it help you to write things down? At one time pupils were expected to spend a large part of their lesson time copying into their exercise books from a text book. They must have learnt something. What they learned, however, would not be known unless they were tested on their knowledge of the content in some way. The combined use of hand, eye and brain does have some effect on learning. Ideally, we should make notes or 'summarise' from texts or lectures, but this is not an easy thing to do without training and practice. Let us perhaps talk of 'rewriting' at this stage, leaving you to develop the skills of note-taking and summary later. The work on note-taking given in this book should help you.

You are intending to learn then by listening, reading, asking questions, discussing with others, teaching and explaining to others and making notes to which you can refer. Then what are you intending to do?

Feedback

Feedback is *so* important. It is a check on what you know already and an encouragement to continue and to develop further. It is an opportunity to correct mistakes or misunderstandings and, paradoxically, is a confidence builder because of that.

Normally we think of feedback in relation to a teacher or tutor. Our questions are answered; our comments are noted and remarked upon; work is marked and written comment tells us how much we have understood and what else we might have done or used. A grade or mark is often given which will give us some indication of where we are in relation to others and to our ultimate goal.

Feedback is also the result of practice, using what we have learned to solve a problem in science, maths and practical subjects particularly. We practise what we have learned, we see how well we could have done by making correct or incorrect answers. We see whether what we have produced actually 'works'. Do not be afraid of incorrect answers. The wrong answer is very useful as feedback. In this way we can see clearly that there is something (a) we did not know, (b) we did not understand, (c) we have misinterpreted, or (d) we have noted down wrongly. Whatever it may be, we can look again at the problem and hopefully solve it. Do not be put off by a 'funny number' answer. It may be right!

Feedback then, enables us to learn more, to extend our knowledge further. Success is pleasant and solving a problem gives a comfortable feeling of self-approval. We all need positive feedback on which to build confidence. We will now be able to study, to develop a more critical approach and to 'argue' with a writer maybe. (Please note, you cannot argue with anyone about anything if you do not have an 'argument' to put forward, i.e. knowledge of what you are talking about.)

You will begin to understand how something can be understood by understanding what it is *not*, as well as what it *is*: the 'silhouette' or 'cameo' idea. A silhouette or cameo gives a clear picture of a profile, a positive image clarified by a negative background on which it is superimposed. Think of that! It is always dangerous to assume when learning that the mutual exclusion of some ideas can be taken for granted. So often they are. When students seem only able to think in the way flow diagrams work, it is a shame. Opening up the mind whilst learning brings much reward in the excitement of developing the ability to think 'laterally': the recognition of connections, associations and links which are not at first apparent. This kind of intellectual development leads to original work which is as exciting for the tutor as for the student. Learning should be exciting. Look up 'Serendipity', but bear in mind that your own 'fortunate discoveries' will not be made entirely by accident, hopefully.

Learning by our mistakes

We can learn from our mistakes in both formal and informal learning. When we first learn to drive, for example, we often make dreadful mistakes, only by chance do we avoid an accident. Such incidents have an effect on our responses, heighten our awareness of the kind of mistake we made and teach us not to make that mistake again. The same applies to formal learning.

Do not just accept corrected work passively. Find out

where you went wrong. What was it that you did or did not do? In maths, check that your work is set out correctly. So many errors arise from work improperly set out. Are your numbers and signs clear? Is it quite clear what questions you have answered? Have you misinterpreted a sign? Misunderstood a question or a rule?

So many students (and people generally) say in despair that they 'cannot do' maths, mistakenly too. Mathematics needs to be learned in a particular way. You must understand one step before you can progress to the next. The nice thing about mathematics is that it is not a matter of opinion, as some other subjects can be. You cannot disagree with anyone about the sum of 2+2.

Consider fractions for example. If you do not understand references to the term Denominator and Numerator you will be lost. You will not understand any work with fractions. You may arrive at some correct answers by chance without knowing how you got there, but they will not be the result of understanding. First things first, then. Learn your terminology, make sure you understand it, apply it and see what feedback you have.

In work involving languages, do you understand the vocabulary used? Do you understand the rules of language use? (See Chapters 8 and 9.) Ensure that you have a good understanding of the terms used in various subjects so that you can use them properly. Most text books will have a 'glossary' of terms to help you. This advice is particularly applicable to the social sciences, sociology, psychology and economics, all of which have their own so-called 'jargon', not to mention Computer Science which has developed many languages of its own.

Remembering

In order to remember and to be able to say a little about

something, we need to know a lot. We also need to be aware of the difference between knowing 'about' or 'of' something and the 'knowing' which is understanding. Be aware that you may well confuse being unable to recall with not having the requisite knowledge in the first place. But you can easily remedy the situation once you are conscious of it. Nevertheless we all experience those moments when we know, but are quite unable, at that moment, to bring our knowledge to the forefront of our minds. Moments of forgetfulness do not mean that we cannot remember; they mean only that at certain times we find ourselves unable to recall something – a name, telephone number or an address – the 'I know your face but who *are* you?' syndrome. 'It is on the tip of my tongue!'

The first thing all students must believe is this: if you have really learnt something and you know it, then it is *still there*, in your mind, your memory, in that marvellous 'computer' we call the human brain. Knowledge and understanding do not slip away like the bathwater. If you believe this, and it is true, you are a long way towards developing a more relaxed attitude. Urgency and distress are non-productive. Calm confidence will help you to remember. We always remember what we *want* to remember (and forget things we wish to forget!). We remember things associated with being hurt or frightened and experiences which give us pleasure, so, we *can* do it. It is believed that no human being has ever used his intellect to its full extent. This applies even to those we think of as intellectually brilliant. Research does show that the more we use our brains the more we can. As with our bodies, whatever our age may be, the more we make use of our faculties, the sharper they will become.

Formal learning, with the intention of learning for retention and recall, is a deliberate activity and requires control on our part. Clarity is important. We cannot learn in a muddle. We need to set out our intended learning clearly, being aware of our final learning goal and being able to set ourselves intermediate learning 'targets' or 'objectives' in the approach to that goal.

You do not 'learn' maths or chemistry, literature or history without first learning how to deal with the parts of those subjects which are relevant (a) to your ability to learn and understand at the time, and (b) to the requirements of the course you are studying. Problems will naturally arise if there is a discrepancy between (a) and (b). Do not let yourself get into a state of confusion or *that* is what you will remember.

Techniques

There are some other techniques which have proved to be helpful to many students as well as the learning by objectives and aims approach. Sometimes we really do need to 'learn by rote' until what we have learned through repetition becomes so familiar to us that we cannot believe we once did not know it.

Techniques to aid information 'retrieval' such as mnemonics, memory jogging, associations, verse, highlighting of text, saying aloud, repetition and chanting all have a part to play in helping us. 'Mnemonics' is a term which refers to any memory aid. It is usually used to refer to aids which are based on the capital letters of words, related to lists, which in themselves have no intrinsic meaning. The letters can be used to make a 'word' which by association triggers recall. This is particularly useful when learning to remember facts which in themselves do not have meaningful associations. Please be aware though that a memory aid is meant to help you, not to give you something else to learn which will take up your valuable time and energy. If the association does not work for you it is not of use to you.

Verses can be helpful. Rhythm and rhyme are easier to remember than straight prose. A verse that is funny is also better than one which is not. In your notes, try highlighting important items using colour. Say the words aloud. Learn as you would a nursery rhyme. Test yourself. Make yourself say what you wish to remember and write it down again.

For those of you who will be expected to write examination essays, try this. Concentrate on a topic at a time. List all the important points within that topic. Highlight them, as above. Number them. What is the total? Note the total number, then, if you wish, sub-divide the items into relevant areas and number these too. How many in each area? Remember the total, remember the sub-totals. Recall of the actual numbers does really help with recall of the information. E.g. 'Point 19 – invasion'. If you can remember say 23 points for your essay topic, you have 23 credits and you have made 23 points which can be marked.

Motivation

All students need motivation (perhaps the 'cue-deaf' do not have this, which would explain their problem!). A well-motivated student has a good chance of achieving what he sets out to achieve. The student with 'intrinsic' motivation, that is a love of learning for its own sake, will find it easier to learn than a student without such involvement. However, we cannot all really enjoy everything we are expected to do all of the time. 'Extrinsic' motivation is not to be denigrated: the wish to get qualifications, to do the kind of work we wish to do, to be financially secure, are all good motives for study. It would be very difficult for someone who hated learning to do well, but for most of us the rewards of study are both intrinsic and extrinsic. That is, fortunately we enjoy most of what we do for its own sake and also we keep going because we hope for a final 'reward'. Motivations are many and varied. The more rewarding our learning the more chance we have of achieving our goals.

Pupils are frequently amazed by how much teachers 'know'. However do they manage to remember all that? The answer is, of course, that once they were like you, learning, learning how to learn, working out ways to recall, assimilating knowledge, developing understanding by continuous reading, listening, noting and getting involved; increasing the depth and breadth of their knowledge by constant application of what is already known to what, as yet, is not so well understood. In other words, making the effort.

The only way to learn, in the end, is to get on with it. However you feel, whether your brain is 'in gear' or not, you must begin. Clutching your pen or book whilst gazing out of the window at the patterns the clouds are making is not learning. It is called daydreaming. Pick up your pen, look at your book, do something – anything. Write your name. You must begin in order to continue.

To sum up
1. Formal learning involves *deliberate* effort on your part. Informal learning is also the result of effort, but unconscious effort.
2. Do not confuse recall with learning.
3. Be confident that you can learn. Think about what you have learned already, think about what you can do (write a list if you like, you will be pleased with yourself!).
4. It is important to learn the basics of any subject in order to progress to more advanced learning.
5. Do not blame yourself if you do not know something – learn it.
6. Practise what you have learned to do.

7. Be actively involved in your learning. Ask, question, listen, look, write and read.
8. Understanding develops through accumulation of knowledge (see 'Some learning theory', page 24).
9. Use all the aids to learning that you can.
10. Do not be discouraged by physical disabilities.
11. Learn how you learn best.
12. Learn by teaching others.
13. Develop an understanding of feedback.
14. Do not fear mistakes.
15. You do not 'forget' anything you have learned even if you cannot recall it immediately.
16. Become more confident about your ability to recall by developing techniques which suit you.
17. Hang on to your 'motivation' to keep going.

3

CONCENTRATION

Definition of concentration: 'intense mental application', 'complete attention'. The definition itself has connotations of great effort, screwed up faces, rigid figures, stiff backs, all the aspects of 'concentration' which, in reality, militate against it. You cannot concentrate if you are actively concentrating on 'concentration'. Now we have settled that, let us see what can be done about developing the ability to concentrate when we work.

Be assured, the ability to concentrate does improve over time and with practice. You must have the will to do so however, otherwise you will not be able to make yourself overcome your initial inertia. Those of you who understand the term 'inertia' will be aware that it applies to an unmoving, still object (a vehicle, before it begins to move, is in a state of 'inertia'). So are you, as a student, as you sit at your desk, your work before you, pen in hand, and before you begin.

Overcoming inertia

Start. Give yourself a push. You must begin whatever it is you had intended or planned to do. In fact, planning to begin a particular piece of work, to read a certain book, chapter or anything else, is the first step towards learning how to concentrate. The second step is believing that you can.

In the chapter on Organising Study Time, you were advised to be well-organised in a practical way, so that you can begin to work without needing to search for any materials that you need. Such organisation will be invaluable for you if you find it difficult at first to develop the level of concentration you would like. Having everything to hand and easily accessible will help you to get started and to overcome your initial inertia.

The above is one way of minimising interruptions as you work. You will need to control these as far as you can. Concentration, once developed, needs to be continuous (not continual, note the difference!) in order to be effective, to change from a superficial to a deeper level.

You cannot *make* yourself concentrate any more than you can make yourself sleep. Insomniacs among you will know that all too well. The harder you squeeze your eyes shut, the more you wriggle around to get comfortable, the more you say to yourself as you lie rigidly in your bed, 'I *will* go to sleep', the less likely you are to do so. Sleep should catch you unawares: one moment you are conscious and the next, asleep. You do not remember actually *falling* asleep, you only know that you must have done so when eventually you wake up! Insomniacs fear not being able to sleep. Do not fear not being able to concentrate.

Concentration is like that. You can slip into a deep level of concentration without realising it is happening – sometimes for a short period, sometimes for so long that you 'awaken' cold, stiff and hungry.

'That's not me,' you may say. 'I can't do that'. Yes, you can. If you are very interested in something, you concentrate. You become absorbed in what you are doing or what is happening. Notice particularly how children become involved in computer games, in play. Their concentration is such that they may not hear anything else that is happening around them. Certainly not the bell for school to resume or the command to go to bed!

Once you have mastered the art of deep concentration, you will find that it becomes easier to achieve. Deaf to all around you, unaware of anything but your work, then you will be able to leave your work temporarily if you need to without losing the thread of what you have been doing. Returning to your work, you will find it increasingly possible to 'slip' back into the concentration mode you have recently left. Rather like returning to ride a bicycle and immediately regaining your balance. To do this, you need to choose your break time when your work is interesting and you feel you do not really want to leave it. Then, you will want to go back to it as soon as you can.

How do you get there in the first place? As has been said, you begin. Even if initially you can only work at a shallow concentration level, you must begin. If you do not start you cannot develop any level of concentration at all. Allow your mind to work for you. Trust it. Most students underestimate the ability they have to use their minds. In fact, perhaps it might be better to say, 'to let their minds operate'. Your thoughts may wander at first, exploring previously learned information to do with the topic you are planning (note, not *trying*!) to concentrate on. Permit your mind to nudge open the doors of memory. Relax into your thinking, explore thoughts that relate to what you are doing when they occur to you. You will find yourself becoming more and more absorbed. In short, you are concentrating.

Difficulties

We have seen that being prepared to work minimises interruption. Certainly, you cannot develop concentration of any depth if you are continually being disturbed or disturbing yourself. For some of you, disruption is a problem. Do what you can.

One of the things you can do is to recognise when it really would be better to stop trying to work and deal with something that may be on your mind. Anything that is of sufficient importance to you to constantly encroach upon your efforts to concentrate, should be attended to. Otherwise, you will feel miserable and unsettled. Get it done, whatever it is. Clear your mind and conscience so that you can apply yourself, single-mindedly, to your planned study. If you are truly disciplined, you will be able to recognise a real need from wishful thinking. The more you practise concentrating, the easier it becomes, the less is your fear of not doing so and the less likely you are to procrastinate. Then, the more likely you are to succeed and feel good. If we feel good about something we like to repeat it.

So far, the concentration we have been discussing is applicable to reading and to written work in situations in which we are in control. Do not neglect the physical aspects of either. Discomfort does affect our ability to be single-minded.

This leads to consideration of lectures and lessons in which the physical aspects of our situation are *not* under our control.

With what do we have to contend? Too much comfort sometimes. Easy, squashy chairs in seminars perhaps, or hard, uncomfortable ones in lectures or lessons. Desks the wrong height for us. Rooms which are too hot or too cold. Daytime sun shining through windows onto us. We feel the need to fidget, wriggle around and move about in these circumstances. Keeping still is very difficult for many people. Concentration becomes even more difficult if the lecture or lesson is inaudible, boring, confusing or too long.

Pity the poor teacher or lecturer who has to maintain the flow of inspiration for longer than he would wish. At least he can move about. You cannot. What to do? Not fall asleep or doze, please, tempting though it may be.

You should already have some knowledge of the lecture, lesson or seminar content. Use this to involve yourself mentally in what is being said or what is happening. Be prepared to take notes and be active. Ensure that you can take notes easily. A clipboard is best as a folder can slip about at awkward moments. Make sure you have a pen that works and a back up if need be.

Try to be as comfortable as you can, so that you are not distracted by the physical discomfort of unsuitable clothing.

Can you see? Can you hear? Sit at the front – not only will you see and hear more but you will be conscious of the fact that the lecturer or teacher can see you and also that students behind you can see you too! You are less likely to fall asleep in these circumstances. There is a limit to your control of such situations but you can alleviate matters if you try.

Positively, you may well find your lessons or lectures inspiring. In that case you will not find concentrating so difficult. It will be easier for you mentally to override any discomfort you may experience. However this may be, the level of concentration needed in those circumstances is different. It is an active, participant concentration that you need. Previously, the needed concentration was one you engineered for yourself. When you doubt your ability to concentrate to the extent needed, remind yourself of the times when you do so: reading an absorbing book, listening to wonderful music, playing music yourself, creating, being involved in something you love doing. You can concentrate then, can't you?

To sum up
1. Recognise and learn to overcome your initial 'inertia'. Give yourself a 'push'.
2. Minimise interruptions as far as you can.
3. You cannot *make* yourself concentrate.

4. Deal with anything that is really bothering you before trying to concentrate.
5. Pay attention to physical comfort.
6. In lectures, sit at the front!

4
READING

There are 39 entries for the word 'read' in the dictionary and 16 for 'reading'. The dictionary also tells us the origin of the word 'read', it is from the Old English 'raëdan', which means to advise or explain. Within the definition of 'read' we are given to understand that it refers to 'comprehension' and 'interpretation' of the written word, to 'undertake a course of study' (as in 'she read mathematics at university') and many more besides.

Within the definitions are some which do not necessarily apply to the written word. We can 'read' signs, 'read' body language and facial expressions, 'read' someone's mind, 'read' a radio message by learning and understanding it, 'read' music and 'read between the lines'. All these definitions imply understanding and interpretation of whatever it is that we have 'read' in whatever way.

What do we do when we read?
The interpretation of printed or written material, 'reading' is an amazing skill which we develop through a combination of teaching and practice. The co-ordination of eye and brain involved in this activity develops to the extent that we become able not only to sound letters to make words (phonics) but also to make sense of these shapes and sounds. We begin to be able to understand the ideas they represent.

Although we do not all become as proficient and highly skilled as some, we must at least have become competent in order to read this. Advanced reading skills become as natural to the reader as do walking and talking. Even if we are not as skilful as that we can still learn to use written materials for our own studies efficiently.

It is natural that when we attempt to make sense of written or printed material that is unfamiliar to us that we can find it difficult at first. This can be either because the vocabulary is new and strange or because the material presents us with concepts that we have not met before. Initially, we may feel that we will never succeed in developing the understanding we need to use this material. This chapter intends to deal with such concerns by explaining firstly, 'what' to read and secondly 'how' to do so efficiently and productively. Thirdly and fourthly, it may be helpful to consider the 'why' and 'where' as well as the 'what' and 'how' of reading.

What to read
When you enrol for a course of study you should be given some indication of the materials and texts you are expected to use. At a basic level you will be told what texts will be used for each subject you are studying and hopefully you will be provided with copies to keep for the duration of your course. This does not always happen, unfortunately, as sometimes books have to be shared with others and sometimes a student is not allowed to take them home. If you are in this situation it would obviously be better if you could obtain copies of your own, copies you could keep and mark. Failing that, this chapter may give you other ideas.

At a more advanced level of study, you will probably be given a reading list for the given subjects of your intended course. You may receive this before term starts and be expected to begin your reading before you have begun your course.

For many students, such a list is a shock. It is normally very long indeed. It is long because the intention of the list is to provide extensive information about the appropriate material which is recommended for your course. Tutors' favourite texts and authors will be included, inevitably, as will their favoured journals and magazines perhaps.

Some students think that they really are meant to read all these books. Be comforted, for you are not. If you did try to do so, you would have no time either to understand them or to do anything else. Apart from that, it is doubtful whether you would be able to find them all, to borrow or to buy. As for buying them all, unless money is no object, it would be out of the question. Books can be very expensive.

Most likely, several references will be indicated as 'essential reading', in which case you can begin with one or two of these, or whichever you can get hold of, either by borrowing or buying. Do not despair if you cannot find a textbook immediately, it will be possible to order one to borrow or to buy. Very good sources of useful and important texts are students who have done the course before you and who are usually only too pleased to sell you their used copies at a reduced price. Texts can be expensive so take care that you do not spend unnecessarily. You may be able to share expenses with another student in your year. Try to invest wisely.

Selectivity
Let us assume that you are beginning a new, exciting course and cannot wait to get started on your reading. At this stage you will not be able to select sensibly from the recommended lists. Begin then, with the 'essentials'.

As the course is new to you, you may find the books you

are expected to read are quite difficult at first. Don't worry. Choose the book you feel most comfortable with and begin with that. To make it easy for yourself, check the vocabulary for difficulty, the headings for clarity and the print for the comfort of your eyesight. Then begin.

This initial 'introduction' to your subject is important. It is the only time you will be recommended to 'begin at the beginning' and work your way through to the end. This does not mean that every word should be carefully studied. Assuming that the book you have chosen from the 'essentials' list is a text that covers your subject in a general way (as it should be, as an 'essential'), you will, by working through it, have developed a general understanding of your future work. You can go on from there. After you have read your book, you should feel far more confident and therefore much more able to be selective about the other recommended readings.

So start simply, as simply as you like. Build on this understanding.

Select your reading

You now need to develop the skill of selecting the books you intend to read and to differentiate between those which will and will not serve your purpose. You also need to be able to select, within the books you choose, those parts you consider will be of use to you.

Please do not think that you must read every word, page, chapter of every book you use. You will not have time to do this and you do not need to do so (the study of particular novels, plays and poetry is, of course, a different matter and detailed study is required in these circumstances).

Most books consist of a title, front cover, back cover, contents page, list of illustrations, diagrams, charts etc. (if there are any), publisher's information page which shows the publication date, reprints and their dates, if any, information about the author (maybe), an index (at the back), and perhaps a glossary of terms. So, before you actually use your book, sort it out.

Sort it out

1. Title, does it apply to your subject?
2. The back cover, the 'blurb' about the book – does this suggest the book may be of use to you? If the answer is 'yes' to the above, look further.
3. Look at the contents page. Do the chapters listed look as if they may meet your needs? All of them? Just some of them? Enough to bother with?
4. Has the book an index? Check this for any particular item you are interested in which may or may not be obvious from the contents page. Is it referenced? If so, how much? Enough to help you?
5. Check the date of publication. This can be important in many subject areas as it indicates how up-to-date the scholarship of the text will be. A popular and therefore normally successful text will also show evidence of *revised* reprints which should include the latest developments.

   Obviously you would not subject 'classic' texts to the same kind of publication scrutiny. You would be referring to them as the 'classics' they are. Very often you will find them referenced in other works, maybe as 'primary sources' even, which leads us to:
6. Bibliography and acknowledgements. These are normally found at the end of the book and are lists of books and other materials used by the author in writing the book. Sometimes it is quite amusing to see how a very small book can credit a immense number of references! Seriously, the bibliography of a good text can point you in

several useful directions for further study. Not just to other books either. As you develop confidence in your ability to select texts and materials, be braver. Use those recommended by all means, but do not underestimate your own ability to recognise the usefulness of something else, by someone else. If a book, or any other reference, alerts you to potential, use it. This is what study is about after all, your individual development.

More 'whats'

There are many other sources of information apart from books, although books usually remain our main resource.

First, we have the main texts, then supplementary texts. Supplementary texts concentrate on particular aspects of a subject and are more specific. They contain information which will illuminate and extend the general information we already have. We should find more detail, more information and therefore more depth in these books when we are ready. The bibliographies of our main texts should lead us to the additional texts. They should also be shown on our reading lists.

Other materials

In addition to main and supplementary texts, you will no doubt be using other materials and sources of information. The value of what you use depends on how you use it. History students for example will need to become familiar with the use of primary sources and must learn to differentiate primary from secondary materials. They should also try to develop a knowledge of historians and their specialities so that they can recognise the importance of references in a journal, magazine or report when they meet them. All subjects will have their specialist periodicals, some will be more academic than others. That does not matter. If you increase your knowledge and understanding whilst you are enjoying your reading, so much the better.

As a student you need to be constantly aware of the potential of many resources. Do not despise simplicity. It is quite possible to find a useful approach, written, pictorial or diagrammatic in materials written for children for example. Your references might also direct you towards 'readings'. 'Readings' are a collection of essays or articles about a subject or topic written by experts. They are often controversial, which is good for your study, and again you do not have to read them all. Select. No doubt you will find yourself referring to reports, 'papers', magazine articles or electronic sources, again written by subject specialists.

Using the Internet
These days anyone can gain access to the Internet – either at home, school, college, university, work, library or at a cyber café. Originally developed as a means of sharing academic research, it is an invaluable tool to today's student.

Web sites dealing with just about every conceivable topic and academic subject may be found by conducting a search on relevant keywords through a 'search engine' (a web site which explores the World Wide Web for pages which contain the keywords you have entered). There are dozens of such search engines on the Net, some of the largest being www.yahoo.com, www.altavista.com and www.lycos.com.

If you know what you are doing, you can often find *just* the piece of information that you are looking for on the Net – if you don't, you can also find an awful lot of information that is not at all what you were looking for! The trick is to narrow your search. For example, if you were writing an essay on the theme of deception in the play *The Importance of Being Earnest* by Oscar Wilde, and you wanted to look for some web pages that might deal with this sort of area, what kind of keywords would you use in a search engine? Entering the keywords 'Oscar Wilde' may give you thousands of results: pages mentioning the name 'Oscar', pages mentioning the name 'Wilde', and somewhere, amongst a lot of useless material, some pages about the playwright himself. But do they deal with the play or topic in question and do you have several hours to spare finding out? Most engines give a variety of ways of searching their databases: default methods are usually simply to look for any document containing one or more of your keywords. It is, therefore, worth checking out the options available at a variety of engines when starting out. Do a bit of comparison and pick the engine and the search technique that you feel happiest with. Before entering keywords, see if the search engine supports different categories and try to narrow your search in that way first. For example, for the above essay, you want something on English Literature, rather than gay rights, theatre reviews or pictures of somebody's cat. Many search engines offer an 'intelligent search' (sometimes called a 'Boolean search') whereby you enter your keywords in a specified way to achieve the most helpful results. The syntax differs from engine to engine, but often entering something like 'Oscar+Wilde+Earnest+deception' will ensure that the search engine looks only for pages that contain *all* of these relevant keywords, so vastly reducing the number of results and increasing your chances of finding something of use.

If you have exhausted several different search engines and *still* can't find anything of real use, it is often a good idea to go to the web site of a good university (somewhere like www.ox.ac.uk) as these sites often publish up to the minute academic work, or, at the very least, point you in the direction of other helpful places to visit on the Internet. Occasionally, academics may respond via e-mail to intelligent, earnest enquiries about their specialist field. Do not, however, insult their intelligence by asking them to complete your work for you!

If you use any information from the Web in your own essays or projects, you *must* acknowledge your source in the proper way – just as you would do had you gained the information from a book or journal. Reproducing material from an electronic source, be it Internet or CD ROM, without proper citation, carries the same penalties as plagiarism from a printed source. Often, teachers or tutors may give extra marks for (or at least be suitably impressed by) the use of many different media of research, so acknowledging use of the Web, in the proper bibliographic form (see page 78), may well prove to be to your advantage.

How to read

You have chosen the book or text you wish to begin with, checked the contents, index, preface, summary and so on, and have decided that it has a lot to offer you. It is wise to have a dictionary handy when you begin so that you can turn for help immediately if you come across a reference or word you do not understand. If you find the first reading too difficult, don't worry, work on, read on, you will soon begin to develop the general 'idea' or 'picture'. Do not make the mistake of struggling on with word after word. If you find yourself doing this, the text is too difficult for you. Find another text which will not give you so many problems. You will not develop understanding if you need to look up several words on every page. Sentence analysis is *not* what you should be doing. You are supposed to be reading to learn.

Bear in mind this story: Once, an eager, ambitious and very naive student was given a text to read. The tutor said, 'Take this and read it and come back to see me and tell me

what it is about'. The text was very difficult, very specialised, the vocabulary was new and strange. The student,
taking up the 'challenge', read each word, struggling to
understand and analyse each page and chapter, made
copious notes and put them carefully in a ring binder. After
some time, having done this, the student triumphantly presented the fat folder and herself to the tutor.

'What did it say?' asked the tutor. The student opened the
folder and began to expound at length. 'No, no, no, there is
no need for all that. All I wanted was for you to be able to
tell me this . . .' And, in *one sentence* the tutor summed up
that awful book! A lesson well-learned indeed.

So, select your reading wisely and do not waste your
precious reading time. Rather, find something that says 'So
and so says such and such, or this and that'. When you know
you need to work in depth, then do so; otherwise, select.

There are several ways to find out if a book is for you.
One is to 'browse'. This means that you read briefly through
the book, turning pages almost randomly, skipping a bit here
and a bit there, stopping for a while to examine something
more closely as a word or sentence catches your eye, and
moving on. You may then find (a) that the book is not what
you really need, (b) that 'browsing' has proved enough, you
have some information, or (c) that you became involved and
have decided to read the text more thoroughly.

'Skimming' a text is a similar process, a rapid glance at
the pages to see if they are potentially useful. Increasingly
you will become more skilful at recognising important
pieces of information as you browse through or skim
through a text.

A further technique is 'scanning'. When we 'scan', we are
being more deliberate in our search for information. Usually
we have a particular question in mind and we are looking for
specific information. In scanning a page or book, we run our
eye quickly down the pages to see if what we are looking for

is there. If we find it, we can stop and use it. If not, we continue to scan. When using all of these suggested techniques we need to be able to pick up 'cues', to see the 'signposts' on these pages which tell us whether we should look more closely. Some signs are obvious and catch our attention more easily than others: differences in typeface, bold or italics, capitals, headings, numbered lists, underlining or colour. Other 'signposts' are linguistic, attracting our attention by the words they use: words such as 'however', 'furthermore', 'finally', 'of course', 'let us consider', 'perhaps', 'it could be said', and so on. All these signposts say 'Pay attention', 'Look at this', 'This may be important/of use to you'.

You will find that, the more you read 'around' and 'about' the same topic, the more easily you will assimilate further knowledge and understanding of it. You will become increasingly more able to recognise and make associations. Your reading and learning will become more meaningful. When you reach this stage, you can more easily differentiate between the levels of reading you need to do. Some of your reading will be in depth, some at a more superficial level: whatever suits your purpose.

Different kinds of 'reading'
We do not just 'read' words, however, in order to learn. Diagrams, charts, illustrations, maps, and graphs can all be helpful to understanding. For some students, information presented in this way is something to be avoided. Others see them as the excellent aid they are. Very often a diagram or chart can give a great deal of information simply and clearly. All students are well advised to learn how to handle and decipher these visual aids to learning. Maps are particularly useful to clarify verbal explanations. Read headings carefully. Make sure that you understand what the illustration

intends to show you. All such inclusions in a text are there for a purpose, they are not there by accident.

Often a diagrammatic explanation can make a point much more clearly than words can do. Think of a genealogical chart (family tree) for example. It is much easier to follow ancestral lines from a chart than from a series of sentences.

The development of the analytical techniques necessary to interpret and decipher information presented in this way has positive value in being transferable to 'in depth' study. You cannot interpret charts casually. You must look at them closely. A further advantage can be when you are able to use such an approach yourself when note-making, note-taking or presenting work. You will save time and also clarify the information for yourself.

Work in depth

As you read, you will be looking for the main ideas in the book and you should also be alert to important details. You may not wish to disrupt your reading by making notes at this stage. Your intention is to develop understanding of the 'general' idea from understanding detail. Remember that, without detailed knowledge, understanding is insufficient and shallow. On the other hand, you must not confuse definition and example. If this sounds confusing, no, it isn't. Understanding what something 'is' or 'is not' is not the same as saying what it is 'like'. Differentiate. Examples illustrate, describe, illuminate; they do not 'explain' in themselves, they contribute towards explanations.

In a properly organised book, each section or chapter will deal with an idea which is part of the main idea of the book. Within sections there will be chapters. Within chapters, there will be paragraphs of varying lengths, extending the idea of the chapter by reference to 'sub' ideas. Pay attention to these. The main idea in a paragraph can usually be found at the beginning or end, often in just one sentence. So you can read your book, developing understanding from the general idea to specific ideas, chapter by chapter and paragraph by paragraph, following the development of information or argument as you do so. Unless you are very short of time it is suggested that you do not make notes at this stage. Do this later, then you will know what it is you need to make notes about.

As your reading skills develop and your subject knowledge increases, you will become more effective, you will begin to evaluate what you read and to judge its worth or usefulness. We do have to accept what we read to begin with, as we know no better at that stage, but by now you may be sufficiently knowledgeable and confident to realise that you do not have to take statements for granted.

Look at the arguments put forward by the author. How far does one author's viewpoint challenge or agree with the viewpoint of another? When is the author stating a fact, or is it an opinion? What do you know of the author's prejudices, leanings, affiliations and so on? Can you detect bias in the work? Consider any evidence put forward to support an argument. Does it make sense? Or is it just a cleverly worded 'smokescreen' to enable the writer to put forward his own viewpoint? Does the author wander off at a tangent, leading you into seemingly important 'irrelevancies' because he wants to include a pet idea that does not really 'fit'? A clever writer can be very convincing with words.

On the other hand, perhaps you have found a text and author you feel you can trust and be comfortable with. The language is clear, content is relevant to your needs and arguments are well supported and considered. Opposing viewpoints are put forward fairly. There is informed comment, the summary is concise and the conclusions acceptable. In this case, even if you feel that you can base your studies on this particular text, you must still explore other avenues of information. You must still support your studies by extending your reading to supplementary works.

Remember to record your reading. It is infuriating to be unable to remember a reference that you know you have used. You may think you will remember the author's name and book title without making a deliberate record but the likelihood is that you will not. The mind plays games with us. We could spend hours looking for 'Wilson' instead of 'Watson'!

We all know that it is very wrong to deface materials we use which belong to a library or to someone else. However, quite often a caustic comment written in the margin by a previous reader can give us food for thought, or make us smile. Sometimes their interest or outrage is so clear to us that we feel we could become involved in discussion. With your own books, your own property, you can of course do this. You can 'discuss' with the author. Agree or disagree, be caustic, outraged, amused, whatever you feel. Be involved.

Do not be attracted to the ideas of speed reading techniques. Research into the effectiveness of such techniques suggests only that the time spent developing them is time lost to learning. Instead, develop the techniques suggested above and use the appropriate technique for your particular purpose at the time.

For example, perhaps you wish to find out about a particular person. Maybe you have found a biography or autobiography of that person but you feel the need for more information, as you should. Perhaps the biography has been written with bias or prejudice. Refer to (a) the chapter headings of books relevant to the time or topic in question, then (b) refer to indexes where the person's name may be referenced, collect the information in 'small pieces' and add these to the information you already have.

At other times you need to read deeply, your purpose being depth of understanding. You will be making an effort at recall by making notes for later reference. Then you will be 'browsing' to see whether the material is for you, casually turning pages, stopping here and there, reading, skipping and moving on. Sometimes you will find it easy enough to skim through a chapter; just one chapter may serve your purpose at that time. Another time you may need to look more closely at two or three chapters or parts of chapters. You have found out what you need to do by your original investigation of contents and index, then by skimming or scanning appropriate sections.

There has been so much emphasis in this chapter on a disciplined approach to the development of reading skills that we seem to have forgotten the most important aspect of all, enjoyment.

Reading can bring so much pleasure to our lives as well as information. The more you read, the more skilful you will become and the more you will enjoy reading. Because your reading is so easy you will feel free to allow yourself time to read for pleasure. The more you do so, the more you will develop your reading skills. It will all become easier and easier. Your vocabulary will grow and with it your understanding and ability to express yourself. Language use will improve, confidence will grow. If you can share your reading experiences with others you can share your enjoyment too.

To sum up
1. Reading must involve understanding.
2. Use your reading lists sensibly. Invest wisely in your texts.
3. Select between main and supplementary texts.
4. Explore a variety of reading materials.
5. Choose texts which you can cope with.
6. Develop the ability to 'read' at different levels of

involvement, according to your purpose at the time (e.g. browse, skim, scan or read in depth).

7. Make full use of contents pages, indexes, bibliographies and other references e.g. glossaries.

8. Be prepared to use information presented in forms other than words (e.g. maps).

9. Develop the ability to concentrate in depth when necessary.

10. 'Argue' with the author. Be involved.

11. Record your reading.

5

NOTE-TAKING, NOTE-MAKING AND SUMMARY

Notes are essential for future reference, for essay and coursework content and, of course, for revision at examination time. Most students, at whatever level they may be working, find note-taking difficult. Many teachers and tutors recognise this and will give notes as handouts or, at a lower level of study, will dictate the notes they wish you to have. However, at any level above this, you will be expected to make and take notes yourself. Only rarely are you taught how to do so. At one time, most pupils were expected to practise 'précis' work in English. This was an excellent foundation for the development of the skills of summary and note-taking. Unfortunately, such practice is not often provided today. If such practice is offered at all it is usually only occasionally, and takes the form of 'in your own words' or 'in not more than (so many) words explain what has been said'. This is not enough to develop the skills you need.

You will need to take and make notes from several sources: texts, lessons and lectures, television, radio, video and any other media you may be using. Therefore you need to be able to record what you wish to use when reading, watching and listening. Techniques for these three experiences are not the same. We will consider the differences shortly.

First let us look at common problems. Problems are particularly acute when students become responsible for their own notes for the first time.

Masses and masses of notes? In our attempt to miss nothing we scribble down everything as we try to 'keep up'. This applies particularly to lecture notes. 'Scribble' or 'scrawl' is the most common problem. We find we cannot read what we have 'written' – perhaps we have forgotten what it was all about anyway – and our notes are meaningless. What *did* we mean? What is that word? Why did we underline that? Or asterisk that? Maybe we need to find some information for an essay. Where is it? Where are those references we feel would be so useful?

Lecture notes

Lectures differ in presentation. Some are purely verbal as a 'lecture' is conventionally understood to be, with the lecturer standing or sitting in front of an 'audience' of students. Sometimes lectures are supported by visual aids of various kinds, wall charts, OHPs, flip charts, handouts, videos and so on. Lectures, unlike videos and static texts, will not wait for you. You cannot press a button on the lecturer and rewind.

The most difficult lecture to deal with is the conventional kind without visual aid support, unless the speaker is very aware of his students' needs. If he is, then he will help you by providing you with the 'cues' you need to make appropriate notes during the lecture. He will emphasise, pause, indicate the importance of a point by repetition and generally point you in the right direction. If he is not so aware, then you must try to do this for yourself. No, it's not easy. Practice will help but at first you will find that you either miss what is being said because you are trying to write *everything* down or a little of everything, so you get lost and left behind, or you wait for 'cues' which are either not given or which you do not recognise. If you are given lecture notes or handouts, then your task is made much easier. Do not just accept them, use them. Make your own notes around them during the lecture. Mark emphases and make your own written comments. Involve yourself in what is being said.

Listen for 'cues' which will indicate points that the lecturer thinks are important. Verbal 'cues' are expressions such as, 'Firstly', or 'in the first place', 'secondly', or 'in the second place', 'it is clear that', 'most importantly', 'more important however', 'nevertheless', 'as well as', 'in addition to', 'an essential feature of' and so on. Be alert to comments like these.

If your lecturer or teacher does not speak clearly, do not despair. Compare your notes and understandings of the lecture's content with another student if you can. If the lecturer or teacher is approachable, do just that: approach him and ask if he can recommend any further reading that would help your understanding of what was being said.

Any handouts will of course be incorporated into your notes file, maybe with your own comments added. Other visual aids will help you remember important points. Diagrams and charts should be quickly copied, as far as possible. Again, compare your results with those of a colleague or colleagues. You will all benefit from clearing up any possible misunderstanding and may even find that, between you, you have gathered together a rather good résumé of the lecture.

If you plan to use radio or television programmes, try to arrange to tape them. If the programmes are 'live' they will not wait for you if you decide half way through that they would be even more useful than you originally thought. It does not matter if you tape something that afterwards you do not need. That can be erased. It *does* matter if you miss half of a programme whilst you are arranging to record it. Taped and videoed programmes are under your control. You can pause, stop, rewind, whatever you want to do, and make your notes at your own pace.

Notes from reading

Reading materials are also static. The only problem you may have is that you may not be able to keep borrowed material as long as you would like. Maximise the length of time you can keep your material by planning ahead and getting to the library first! When given a reference, go straight away to get it: let others go for coffee and a break.

The nice thing about books is that they give you your heading, sub-headings and contents. The only problem is sorting all this out.

Let us take a main text as a first example as you will need to make more notes from that than from a supplementary text. First, note the title and author and any other information that you may need later for your bibliography (see page 78). Then, if you need to, read the whole book (see Chapter 4 on reading). Work through chapter by chapter. Use the chapter headings for your notes. As you read each chapter, note how each paragraph contains a main idea. Note that idea. If you feel that any examples given will be useful memory 'joggers', note these too, but bear in mind the point made previously that examples are *not* explanations.

If you have decided that you do not need to use the whole of a book again, follow the advice in the chapter on reading. Work as above if you only need to use one or two chapters or a few chapters or parts of chapters. If you are looking for specific information, use the index. Note the page numbers of the index references you wish to look at. Write them down. This will save you going backwards and forwards through the book. Collect all the page numbers first. Then all you have to do is to read, skim or scan the appropriate pages, noting any important points you wish to keep for future reference. Always note the title and author and publishing details. If you work from a book of readings or collected essays, note the titles of different contributors and authors, if you use any. Always, also, acknowledge quotations – even in your notes. It is easy to think that you actually wrote these words yourself when you did not, especially if you become immersed in the subject and the words you have been reading are buzzing about in your head. You must always give credit in your work and you will not know when to do so unless you give credit in your notes.

A useful technique to develop is that of a personal shorthand. Those of you who can write in shorthand are fortunate. Most of us are not able to do this, so we must develop our own. You are not being advised to contrive a whole shorthand system of course, just a useful collection of easily understood abbreviations, some of which will be universally known, such as e.g. and etc., and others which could be peculiarly yours. 'Peculiarly' does not mean 'odd' or 'funny', just specifically yours in relation to the subject or subjects you are studying and your own understandings. We are used to using abbreviations in maths and science all the time: plus and minus, multiply, subtract, formulae for substances and processes. So why not in other subjects too for our convenience? How about Δ for 'change', Δng for 'changing' and using + for 'also' or 'as well as', or 'in addition to'. You can easily develop your own as you progress in note-taking. Make sure though that you can read them.

Your note-taking will become very personal and will develop from *how* you learn and the demands of your subject. You must be able to use them later on. That is what they are for. Make sure that your notes, in whatever form, are *well-spaced*. An incoherent jumble of words will not help you.

There are other ways of recording information apart from

notes written in shorthand and/or straight prose. For some topics you may find diagrammatic notes very useful. 'Spiders', 'sprays', 'concept maps', word and picture diagrams of all kinds can clarify information which otherwise could be confusing. The looser nature of a 'spider' can always be further worked into a 'spray' for example. Further work can turn either into prose with headings or into any form required.

So often books recommend the use of various techniques without actually showing us what they are. It is assumed we know. Perhaps we don't. So, for those of you who do *not* know what is meant by sprays, spiders, concept maps and so on, here they are.

Spiders, sprays and concept maps

A spider diagram is rather like 'brainstorming'. The ideas do not have to be in order. You will usually find that you wish to draw 'legs' from 'legs' for further associated ideas and this can lead to muddle. So, leave yourself plenty of space.

A spray is what it sounds like: ideas spray in a more con-

Fig. 1 A spider diagram

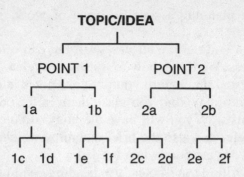

Fig. 2 A spray

trolled way from a central source of information developing direction as conceptual extensions.

'Concepts' are just ideas. Concept 'maps' are similar to spider and spray diagrams. However, we think of concept maps as showing more structure than spiders as they relate several topics to a main idea, whereas a 'spider' can be used for one of the topics with legs showing points and sub points. You may find it easier to sort out your ideas this way or you may find that these techniques are most helpful to

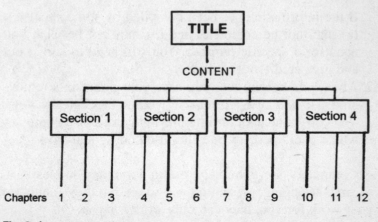

Fig. 3 A concept map

you when planning a specific piece of work, such as an essay.

Skeleton outlines are all very well but can often become meaningless. We forget how to 'flesh our skeletons out'. So, it is suggested that before you put your notes into diagrammatic form of any kind you make them in the conventional way. In this way, you will have the body of notes to which you can refer and also the brief diagrams which will hopefully jog your memory when needed.

When writing your notes, use headings and numbers for both headings and points. Remember to leave *space*. Use italic or bold for headings.

Colour can also be so useful. Use it in a straightforward way to highlight different aspects of topics. You will then be able to see at a glance, all the points related to a particular aspect within a topic.

Apart from being useful, colour looks nice and can make you feel more secure. You can *see* the information is there.

Those of you who are sufficiently fortunate to have access to a computer will of course be using this aid to learning and note-taking, but please remember that:

1. If the information has been compiled by someone else it (a) may not be complete, and (b) may not be what you need for a specific purpose. You still need to sort it out and give credit to its author.
2. Always make sure that you save your notes on a removable disk *and* keep a print-out in case of technical failure.
3. You can spend a lot of time playing games on a computer which could perhaps be better used doing real work.

Computers are extremely useful for many processes – sorting, arranging, presenting and so on, but they cannot *do* your work for you, they can only work for you.

Filing your notes
To begin with, let us assume that your notes are on paper. This being so, the most efficient filing system is the simple one of a loose-leaf binder. Use different colour-coded dividers if you can for topics within topics. Each subject really needs a binder of its own and these can also be colour-coded. The advantage of this system is that it is flexible: you can add material at any time and you can put it where you want it to be. If you are really efficient, you can make yourself a contents page for each binder. That will not really be so necessary though if you colour-code. In your binder, include all the handouts you have been given, or you could make a separate 'handout' file, still colour-coded, so that you can find information. You must be able to find your way around your system.

If you begin with the above system you will then be able, at the appropriate time, to condense it into various other forms for easy reference. For revision purposes, when examinations are very close, you will probably find your binders too full of information for easy reference. By this time, however, you will have prepared your original notes for quick, pre-exam scanning (see chapter on examinations).

Use your original notes for coursework and essay writing. You should have the time at that point to work in depth and at length. Examinations are a different matter. For examinations you need a different approach to your records.

Examination notes
This is the time to condense. As you revise, you need to make your organised notes more immediately accessible. You do not *have* to do this of course, but you will find that, as well as making it easy to revise quickly the night before an examination, the very process of rewriting your notes as you condense them will help your learning and therefore

your ability to recall. Not only that, the summarising process itself will show you which points are more important than others. At this stage you really cannot afford to spend time on unnecessary work.

There are several ways in which you can put your notes into a more convenient form. One is simply to summarise what you have done already, keeping the same filing system but condensing the information into a smaller space. Another is to create a card index system. If you do this you will need to decide on the practicalities of filing the cards. Most often, a box file is the most useful. These can, however, be surprisingly expensive. If you are an impoverished student you may not wish to do this. If you do, make sure that your system *is* useful, not just pretty. Cards can be quite small, so you will need to be able to summarise your information well. Your system *must* be flexible, so that you can add to it as needed. Use colour again here, either by marking the cards or by using differently coloured cards. Check that what you have written or noted really does serve to trigger your recall. Be prepared to go back to your original file to support your revision if needed. Make as much use of diagrams, maps and abbreviations as you can. All of these techniques will help you to condense. Link associated concepts and knowledge by colour or number, or a combination of both. You want to be able to find relevant information easily, see the whereabouts of related information quickly and know where to find further information from your original notes if you need them.

Having worked at note-taking and note-making, what of summary? Is it the same? Well, almost; a summary is a 'summing up' in fewer words of something that has been written or said. 'To sum up' is a phrase often used by lecturers and teachers (one of your 'cues' in fact). You will see that all the chapters in this book have a 'summary' at the end. This is done to help you, to save you from re-

reading a chapter if all you want is to be reminded what it is about.

A list is the most clear form of summary. A summary in prose still needs to be 'deciphered'. A list can also be numbered. Numbers are easier to remember than (a), (b) and (c). In fact we automatically transfer (a) into 1 and (b) into 2 when we work this way. Numbered lists also have a total which we can easily remember and which will serve to remind us of the separate points which add up to this total.

Finally, for your notes to be of use to you they must be personal to you. You will find that working from another's notes is quite difficult. We all think differently, our perceptions cannot possibly be the same. Even when standing side by side, looking at the same object, we do not see it the same way.

So, as you have been advised in other chapters to make your work your own, to be involved, do the same with your notes. You are more likely to learn from them, and therefore be able to recall what you have done, if your notes really are your own.

To sum up

1. The techniques for note-taking from the different sources are themselves different.
2. Look and listen for 'cues' in lectures, make your own notes on any handouts.
3. Maximise the use of any visual aids.
4. Work with fellow students to compare your notes.
5. Record television or radio programmes. You can always erase them if they are not needed.
6. Differentiate between note-taking from main and supplementary texts.
7. Always note titles and quotations as you work. You will *not* remember them.

8. Develop a personal shorthand (make sure you can read it!).
9. Use diagrammatic notes where appropriate.
10. Use colour.
11. Leave space, don't crowd your notes.
12. Have back-up for computer notes.
13. Choose a flexible filing system.
14. Condense at revision for examination time.
15. Summarise by listing.
16. Make your notes your own.

6
WRITING AN ESSAY

A disciplined and consistent approach to coursework essay writing and other forms of presentation contributes more towards final success than may be thought. A good essay, the result of well-researched and understood information, does not only produce a satisfactory short term result, mark or grade, but is also good practice for examination essays. All the reading, note-taking and other preparation considered so far, which has been done in an organised way, is of inestimable value in the long term. A good essay, full of content, is itself useful as a revision aid. With luck, the same or a similar question will appear in the examination later. How useful that can be! The technique of essay writing can be learned with the will to do so and, as with all things, practice improves performance.

This chapter will be concerned with the way in which *title analysis* can be developed as a technique which is applicable to all titles and disciplines. However, it must be stressed that all students must accept the need for thorough learning, note-taking and preparation before the essay is even begun in draft form. It is assumed that for most students an essay will be set on a topic already studied to some extent. If this is not the case, reference to previous chapters should be of help.

Work with students of differing abilities and at all levels shows that there are worries and problems shared by all:

worries about what to include, what to leave out, how to begin, when to end, how to 'answer the question'. How do you cope with all the notes you have made? Why is it that, after a great deal of hard work, writing all that you know, you get a poor grade or, at least, a disappointing one? So often worries like these result in a sort of 'work paralysis', a situation in which even the best of students can find themselves. This can lead to delay in beginning the necessary work and eventually to inadequate work, hurriedly done to meet a deadline. There must be time to do work properly, calmly and with the confidence that comes from knowing what we are doing. There must be time for a draft, a revised draft and then the final version. Hurriedly written with a deadline to meet, a poor essay results.

A piece of cake or 'Answering the Question'

Analysis of an essay title for the purpose of answering the question can be compared to understanding and then following the instructions for a recipe in a cookery book. A recipe will give the name (title) of an intended outcome, a list of ingredients (content) needed and the method of preparation best suited to achieve the wished for result (instructions). Many things can be made with eggs, flour and milk, not just pancakes. Different dishes need more or less of the same ingredients in differing, related proportions, and often the addition of other ingredients in varying quantities. So is it with an essay. Information needs to be arranged in different ways to answer questions presented in different ways. The same information or content will need to be rearranged, emphases altered, points added, points left out. The extent to which an essay question is satisfactorily answered depends on the extent to which the particular demands of a particular question are recognised. To continue with the analogy, a cookery book will give detailed instructions concerning what ingredients to use, the order in which they are to be used and how to use them. Similarly, most essay titles will do that too. The detailed instructions will be in the title and we can learn to see them. Paradoxically, the most difficult title to deal with is sometimes one which is very short: maybe a single word title with the instruction to 'Comment' or 'Discuss'. This is the equivalent of being told to 'make a cake'. In order to obey this instruction we would have to know a great deal about baking, particularly about cake-making, so that we could ourselves provide the list of ingredients and other instructions that the book has not given us. Knowledge and experience are necessary to do this. So is it with an essay. The easiest title to deal with is often one which contains a great deal of information in many words. A short question must be extended to be answered. A long question has the extension and therefore the answer, within it. Most students would, if given the choice, be well advised to choose what is, at first glance, an apparently horrifying question. This choice applies particularly to examination situations in which any student, however confident and able, will find himself under pressure. This advice will make more sense when we come to actual title analysis further on.

When you receive an essay question your first response should be, 'What is it about? Do I know enough? Have I already got the necessary references and notes that I will need? Are my notes easily accessible? Can I begin to plan straight away?' If your answer to these questions is 'Yes', that is very good; if not, then making and organising your notes must be your first priority. (See previous chapters for help with this.)

Next, read your notes. Will the notes you have already be sufficient for your purpose? Do you need an extra 'ingredient' or 'ingredients' that your notes do not yet provide? Do you understand what you are being asked to do? How many words are expected? Find out if you do not know. The length of the work helps you to organise the content. Your time is precious, do not waste it. At this stage of study you should know approximately how many words you write to a page. This knowledge will guide you towards your final draft. Be aware that for the final essay to be of a good standard three or four times as many words as needed for the final result must be written during preparation. There needs to be an original draft, an amended draft and then the final piece of work. All of this takes time so allow yourself plenty if you can. Of course, this approach does not apply to examination conditions or when working to time in class or at home. However, you will find that working in this way will teach you an immense amount, not only about the subject in question, but also how you can cope with answering questions on it. Practice like this when you are not working under pressure will help you to work with maximum efficiency when you are.

Having assembled our 'ingredients', we now need to see what 'method' we are asked to use to achieve the result we want. Within the essay instructions we should be able to find clues to help us decide on the proportions, emphases and parameters of the content to be used in the answer. Let us now consider some commonly found instructions and give some thought to what they actually mean.

An essay at an advanced level of study needs to be more than a piece of writing 'about' something. It needs to meet a particular requirement suggested by the instructions given. Expression of an idea or an opinion in the first person should be avoided. It is considered improper to write 'I think' or 'In my opinion' even if you are asked, 'What is your opinion of?' or 'What do you think is?' or something similar. Such an approach is only permissible for the less academic or younger student who does not know better, or, at the other end of the scale, highly qualified academics or intellectuals who are positing a thesis and who are felt to have the right to do so. We have not yet earned that right.

What forms then can our instructions take? We can be asked to 'Account for . . .', or to 'Write an account of . . .', which is not an invitation to write a simple narrative, although of course a narrative would be better than nothing at all. We need to recognise that an 'Account' is more than that: it is a report, a description and explanation of something that happens or has happened. There is a difference between writing 'about' something and explaining it. Other instructions can ask us to 'Consider', to 'Comment' or to 'Criticise'. When we 'consider' something we have to think carefully about it. The idea of judgment is involved and this means that we need to look at both sides of the question and be able to provide both description and discussion. If asked to 'Comment' we are being asked to explain, to criticise, observe and remark on something. To 'Compare and Contrast' we must be able to write about similarities and differences, how things are the same and how they are different. Criticism involves judgment, analysis and evaluation. When we evaluate we assess the value, worth, usefulness or importance of something. Sometimes an essay question will ask, 'What evidence is there for . . . ?' To answer this we need to be able to provide data to support our argument, to know what has been said about it and give reasons for believing something to be true or not. Asked to 'Describe', we are expected to give an account which includes an explanation. 'Discuss' requires us to debate or to consider or to have a 'conversation' about something. A debate involves reference to all relevant points. 'Distinguish between . . .' asks for a response which recognises differences and similarities. A common mistake here is to give only one side of the argument, conveniently forgetting the other, either because less is known about it or because time is short or because it 'doesn't matter'. But it does. We can be asked to 'Illustrate' our answer which means that relevant examples are expected. Here, we can use analogy to assist our explanation and clarify what we mean and what we have said. As we have seen, it is not wise to have one set approach in our minds to a particular topic within a subject area. We can be asked to show our knowledge in many different ways which, although they may have much in common, are not exactly alike. The same content or information needs to be presented with differing emphases, relationships and proportions. Ensure that you always understand what it is that you are being asked to do.

Mind your language!

For some, writing, reading and the use of words comes easily. For others it can be a considerable problem. There is help however for everyone.

Be comfortable with the sentences you write and the words you use. Short and simple sentences are best if you have difficulty writing your ideas down. Long sentences can become uncontrolled and confusing unless you can punctuate well. Try to develop a style which is pleasant and easy to read. Develop an understanding of punctuation as far as you can. Keep it simple. Do not use punctuation that you do not understand. If apostrophes are a problem, learn the basic rules of their use. Increase your vocabulary and the way in which words are used by reading as much as possible. Use a dictionary and a thesaurus. Use words correctly (look up 'malapropism' in the dictionary). Be aware of the difference between formal and informal language: informal language, that which is used in everyday situations, has no place in formal essay work. Avoid slang, jargon, cliché and idiom unless they are directly relevant to the work in question, as they can be in Literature or Language work. Do not make jokes! Try to avoid repetition as you begin new sentences.

Beginnings such as 'However', 'Perhaps', 'Maybe', 'It could be said', 'Research suggests . . .' should make your work less repetitive and should also help to avoid the dreaded 'I'! Take note of sentences and style that you meet in your reading and learn from them. Correct spelling and punctuation make work easier to read. They go a long way towards creating a good impression. Teachers and tutors appreciate the effort a student makes to present work well; it makes their job more pleasant. So always check your work for errors.

Different approaches are needed for coursework and timed or examination essays. Time should have been allowed for you thoroughly to research and plan a course-work essay. References should be noted and relevant quotations used where appropriate. Timed essays in class or private study do not allow the same luxuries of content planning or reference and quotation use. It is good if the student has researched the topic so well that references and quotations come readily to mind so that they can be used in these situations too, however you will not be expected to achieve the same standard of scholarship in such circumstances. This does not mean that a more casual approach is allowed! What it does mean is that a student who has worked and prepared really well, should be able to apply his knowledge and question-answering skills to the best of his ability, even under pressure. There is no easy way to do this, only by working sensibly beforehand to gather the knowledge and develop the skills you need.

All essays, at whatever level, have a common basic structure. For beginners, we say that they have a beginning, a middle and an end. Later we refer to an introduction, expansion of the information and finally a conclusion. All essays also consist of a series of paragraphs of differing lengths. Each paragraph needs to contain a thesis (idea), a development of that thesis and a link to the next paragraph.

The structure of an essay plan should show the student how the paragraphs in his essay should be arranged. Such a plan is essential to order paragraphing, and therefore content, coherently. This is why *title analysis* is such a useful tool and why the development of this skill is of paramount importance. Paragraphs related to the structure of your essay plan will coincide more or less with the pattern of analysis you have made and will sequence your ideas in order for you.

There are several analytical approaches to essay planning. The one favoured here is straightforward analysis of the wording of a question. This approach is particularly useful in timed situations as it is a method which gives you some control at the outset.

A single approach is however not always the answer for everyone. Some will prefer 'diagrammatic', 'tabular' or 'spider' approaches. All can be useful in relation to particular questions at different levels. It is felt though that there is less likelihood of meandering and irrelevancy if a tighter, analytical approach is used.

Giving credit
If you use someone else's ideas in a piece of written work, whether you read them in a book, on a CD ROM or from a web site, it is very important to give proper credit to the author, even if you are only vaguely referring to his work, rather than directly quoting him.

At a lower level, you may only be expected to give a list of the books that you have used (a bibliography) at the end of your writing. However, those of you at college or university may also need to provide notes within your writing. Different institutions use different conventions for such things but, as a rule, the number for the note should appear after the final punctuation mark of the sentence in which the reference appears. The note should be numbered to concur with this mark and be presented either at the bottom of the page in question (a footnote) or at the end of your essay, chapter or section (an endnote). As well as using these notes to acknowledge the source of your information, you may also use them to add interesting 'asides' which are connected to your subject matter, though not strictly relevant to your argument.

The way that you are expected to present the citation of the sources of your information in your notes and bibliography may differ from institution to institution – some places may not insist that you use any particular convention at all; others may prescribe one method and one method only. If your teachers have not told you how to present the information, use a style that suits you, but *be consistent*. When citing the use of a book, you need to mention:

1. The author's name.
2. The title of the essay/chapter/section within the book (in double quotation marks).
3. The title of the book (underlined or in italics).
4. The name of the general editor of the book (if applicable).
5. The place of publication – just the town or region will suffice.
6. The name of the publisher.
7. The year of publication.
8. The edition number and volume number (if applicable).
9. The numbers of the pages used.

The information for numbers 5, 6, 7 and 8 may be found in the first few pages of the book (in this book you can see it on page 4). So if, for example, you were to use a quotation from *this* book, your inclusion and footnote might look something like this:

In her excellent guide to preparing for exams, *The Exam Secret*, Barbara Brown says that, in order to avoid the penalties of plagiarism, one must give proper credit to all the sources that one has used in one's work.[1]

At the end of your essay, you should list *all* of your sources again, in the same way, in an alphabetised bibliography.

To sum up
1.   Allow yourself adequate time to prepare.
2.   Any title can be analysed.
3.   Become familiar with terms which tell you how you are expected to respond.
4.   Have well-prepared notes available.
5.   Mind your language. Refer to chapter 8 if necessary.
6.   Learn how to structure and plan your essay.
7.   Use the different analytical approaches suggested to decide which approach works best for you.
8.   Be prepared to write more than one draft.
9.   Check your work for errors.
10.   Give credit to your sources and refer to them in the proper way.

---

[1]Brown, Barbara. "Writing an Essay". *The Exam Secret*. Tadworth: Elliot Right Way Books, 2000: pp78–79.

7

ASSIGNMENTS, COURSEWORK AND DISSERTATIONS

The conventional essay is still a very important part of the examinations faced by most students. Today, however, we often find ourselves also expected to present some of our work in other forms as well. Modular courses for example have become increasingly popular. Some of those do include a written examination paper as part of the assessment procedure, but also provide an opportunity for ongoing coursework which can be completed over a longer period of time. At one time, this kind of examination arrangement would be found only at under-graduate and post-graduate level.

In modular courses, the final grade awarded includes marks and grades given for coursework assignments and any timed examinations combined. Sometimes written papers are given at the end of each section of coursework. At other times one written paper will examine all the sections of the course together at the end.

The demands made on students by these arrangements are different from the demands of conventional examinations. For one thing, students need to maintain a steady and consistent approach to all their work throughout the course. It is not possible to work towards a final effort; the effort must be on-going. There are advantages as well as disadvantages to this approach. Individual students find one approach suits them better than another. It is argued that dividing the work between assignments and written examinations gives all students an opportunity to work in a way that suits them best.

Different arrangements of modular courses can be as follows:

1. You study a series of 'modules' or short courses on different topics within the same subject. At the end of this you either have an examination and/or are expected to present a coursework assignment. Assessment can be ongoing throughout the course for each separate module or can culminate in one final assessment at the end when all modules have been completed.

   The advantage is that you know where you are as you progress through the course and, once completed, you know that that piece of work is over and done with. However, you cannot afford to miss a module or any part of the assessment procedure. You may also find that your earlier work is much less mature than the work done later on. Marking and assessment should take this into account, but does not always do so.

2. A combined assessment/final examination. This approach intends to provide students with the opportunity to experience at least one form of work which suits them best. Students who are very nervous about examinations will welcome the opportunity to gain marks by working in a more leisurely way, without the intense pressure examinations can create. However, do remember that working to a deadline creates a pressure of its own. Self discipline and organised study are as necessary here as for conventional examination preparation. Difficulties can also arise

if you are expected to present several assignments within a short space of time for different subjects. This can happen if your tutors or teachers are not as organised as they should be. Look out for this. Mention it and *organise* yourself.

3. A wholly modular course without examinations. This can take several forms and can be assessed in several ways. Again, the student is aware of his level of progress throughout his period of study and must, as before, maintain a steady work effort over a long period of time. Unfortunately, you cannot 'rescue' your grades by improving your final result by a brilliant examination paper!

Assignments

Assignments fall into two categories: those which you are given and those which you are allowed to choose. Clearly any choice approved will relate to the subject you are studying.

At an advanced level of study you will, of course, have greater freedom of choice and will probably be expected to incorporate some kind of 'research' in your final product. Degree 'assignments', usually referred to as 'dissertations', are expected to show a level of originality and scholarship that is not looked for at a lower level. At whatever level you are studying, however, the *approach* to your work should be the same.

Forms of assignment

Firstly, we have the essay which has been dealt with separately (see Chapter 6, page 71).

Secondly, there is the short format written assignment or essay. For this you are given word or space parameters. By this is meant that you are told the maximum and minimum word length of the expected work or you are actually given a space on a page in which to do your writing. Because they are shorter, you may be asked to do more of these than you would if they were longer.

Because an essay is short, this does not mean that you say 'less'. Indeed, you need to be even more succinct, concise and to the point. You cannot afford to digress or wander from the point at all. Within the limitations you have been given there is no room to waste words. Your structure must be tight and you must be sufficiently disciplined to deny yourself the pleasure of demonstrating your knowledge any more than is necessary to answer the question. Yes, it is difficult to do this well. The best way is to make a list of all the points you believe you should write about from your original, loose notes. Decide on the order in which you will deal with these points. Write them in order. Number your list. Work from number one. This way you will be able to control the number of words in each part and, at the same time, you will be able to see if what you say can be shortened or lengthened. By removing unnecessary and adding important information you will maintain the sense of what you are saying.

Purpose
It is important that you recognise the purpose of what you are being asked to do. Keep this in mind as you plan and work. The purpose of your assignment will determine the format as well as the content. Just as you would not (I hope!) consider using pictures to illustrate a conventional essay answer, so you would not write up a report, project or case study in continuous prose. Instead, you would divide your work into sections using appropriate headings. Maybe you would also use maps, diagrams and other

forms of illustration as well.

As with essays, some assignments can help you by containing the suggested structure in their title, or, because of their purpose, the appropriate format will determine the structure. The structure of your work is vitally important. You may have an excellent overall idea of what you wish to do but, if you cannot put the separate parts together to make sense, your understanding is of little use. Without structure your work will be incoherent and formless. A body without a skeleton in fact: loose, floppy and unrecognisable in shape.

Let us now look at one kind of possible assignment which has to be structured because of what it is – the report.

Reports

Perhaps this is the easiest kind of assignment to deal with, on the surface that is. Having previously done the 'research' necessary (more about that later) for the content or subject matter of your report, you need then to:

(a) State the purpose of your work.
(b) Say how it was done, or what was done, and where.
(c) Report on your findings or results.
(d) Conclude by discussing your findings and referring back to (a), the purpose of your report.

Depending on what you have been asked to do, you may also need to consider possible recommendations in relation to the findings and their connection to the original purpose.

Remember, a report deals with *facts*. Any argument or conclusion arising from it *must* rest on factual information. We are all familiar with the idea of police reports for example, and are aware that it is the correct and accurate presentation of the facts which leads to an acceptable conclusion based on them. So too with your work. The format also should be an arrangement of your material which speaks clearly for itself, with appropriate headings, sub-headings and references.

Hopefully, you will find that any reports you are expected to write will be based on experiences which you can easily handle: geographical, archaeological and historical field trips, for example, from which you have already made notes (of course!). Having made your notes, you will need to organise them for your report. If you are lucky, you will perhaps have been given a pre-printed format to complete. In this case your work is simplified.

If not, you must arrange your information yourself using the suggested headings given here and mark your notes for relevance. Use colour coding if you like. Then all you have to do is to arrange the same colour information together and decide what to do with it. Everything is easier if handled in small portions to begin with. It is then up to you to put your jigsaw pieces together.

'Project' as an assignment

One of the most enjoyable learning experiences can come from working on a 'project' either given to you by teachers or tutors, or chosen by yourself. It can also be problematic.

As with a short essay title, you will need to structure the work yourself. Before your imagination can be allowed to wander in many attractive directions, you must arrange a structure in which it can do so profitably. If the title you are using does not in itself give you clear parameters, you must create them.

Where to start? Have a brainstorming session using any form of note-making that suits you best. Then, as with any other work, use a textbook resource for main ideas and supplementary texts for extensions. Make notes. Try to give your 'spider' (see page 64) some coherence. Where do you want to go? (If you find you have an appallingly messy spider and you can make no sense of what you have done – begin again.)

You should by now have some idea of your direction, of the line you wish to take. Make yourself a 'concept' map (see page 65). Extend each concept into a separate 'spider' diagram. Then you can begin to plan. Outline what you intend to do. As you will probably have some time allocated for your work you may find that inspiration leads you along many previously unknown but fascinating pathways.

If, when you have reached a certain stage in your assignment, you find that, despite your careful planning, you are overwhelmed with material that you would love to use but cannot organise, do this. Instead of trying to sort it all out in your mind, or by writing even *more* on paper, do it physically. Find enough space to spread your work out. Arrange it into piles of associated ideas that you have planned for your separate parts or sections. You will then be able to see quite easily what goes with what, where things are and how your material can be ordered. It is particularly helpful now to have colour coded your planning notes.

Unlike an essay, project work lends itself satisfactorily to many different forms of presentation. If time allows, illustrate your work with artwork, with diagrams, maps, pictures, cartoons, colour. Such inclusions should not be extraneous additions to your work but should be integral to it. They should contribute by explaining, illustrating and clarifying what you are also saying in words. Very often, such inclusions can show, far more effectively than words can, how something actually works, how it is structured, how one thing relates to another or what it looks like. You will still need words to express your abstract ideas, to evaluate, to discuss and conclude. Illustrations cannot do that for you but they can be an invaluable aid to your explanation. Apart from the practical value of illustration, consider also the pleasure given both to yourself and the assessor by a beauti-fully presented piece of work.

Obviously, with so much freedom to work as you wish, you will use that freedom to investigate as many different aids to learning and sources of information as you can. Almost 'anything goes', unless you have been told other-wise. Remember, though, that this indulgence can only be allowed to extend so far. You *must* keep to the stated aim of your work. The finished product *must* relate to your title. Experience has shown that a minority of students commonly do two things in these circumstances. Firstly, they enjoy what they are doing so much and make it look so pretty that they actually say very little or even nothing of consequence. Secondly, in their desire to put forward a belief or strongly held viewpoint, they construct an 'oblique' project, one which is not directly relevant to the topic under consider-ation but vaguely associated with it. The topic is used in this case as a 'vehicle' for a viewpoint. Neither approach will do.

Research

Mention has been made of 'research', a much misunder-stood and misused term. What does it really mean? The meaning of 'research' is to seek, to look for, to investigate systematically, to collect information. Sounds easy.

No, it really is *not* so easy. The subject is specialised and needs to be taught and studied as such. Students who wish to do so are advised to investigate further by themselves. It is possible, however, to look at the term briefly and to explain why the claim to have 'done' research at any level should be treated with caution.

The first question to be asked is 'why research?' You will find that the purpose often affects the conclusion. This alone should make us wary. In Chapter 4, students were advised to be aware of prejudice and one-sided arguments. Some research is done in order to 'prove' something the researcher wishes to be so. Hence the use of 'evidence' and 'facts' which support the argument put forward in the first place. The most reliable research is that which sets out to 'prove' that something is *not* so but, after many attempts, cannot do so. Rather like the cameo or silhouette idea on page 30? If you can 'prove' that something is *not*, then you are very close to being able to say what it *is*.

Acceptable research requires a level of skill and training that is appropriate only to advanced degree level or post graduate work. If you are depressed by this, don't be. It is unlikely that at this stage of your education you will be expected to conduct research at any but a very simple level. Having accepted that, there is still no excuse for involving ourselves in 'research' that is meaningless. What are the pitfalls for the inexperienced student who is expected to 'do research'?

At first glance, finding out about something seems to be very simple. You ask questions using a questionnaire. It is very difficult to formulate a good questionnaire. A questionnaire should give us answers which we can collate and use for a conclusion. Unless you are very conscious of *what* you are asking and *why* you are asking it, your work will lack the rigour which would make any findings worthwhile. It is only when we begin to examine what was actually done, and what has been said about what has been done, that we realise that nothing much has been done or said at all! This is very often the result of reliance on an inadequate questionnaires. Questionnaires should provide opportunities for answers which (a) relate usefully to the research question itself, and (b) can be collated, that is, put together afterwards for analysis and eventual conclusion. It is amazing how often questionnaires ask questions which cannot be answered. How often have you been asked such questions?

Inadequate research will inevitably lead to inadequate

conclusions. Inadequate conclusions mean that we have wasted our time. Learn how to differentiate between questions that work and those that don't work, between 'closed' and 'open' questions. An 'open' question is one where the respondent can make up his own answer without restriction. 'Closed' questions are much easier to collate but are limited in scope. For example: 'Are there fairies at the bottom of your garden?' Add up the 'yes' and 'no' answers, present them as a percentage of the total number of persons questioned (the 'population' questioned). You can then say that 'such' a percentage of the population questioned said that there *were* fairies at the bottom of their gardens and the other percentage said not. However, you *cannot* say that either the *majority* of people generally do not have them at the bottom of theirs or that the minority do. Neither can you say that they *think* so, or do *not* think that they do, because that is not what was asked and they may be telling lies.

Be careful. Choose your 'population' carefully. Account for anything that could make a difference to what you eventually say. For example, age, sex or any other group to which people can belong.

At a very simple level, school children can keep a tally of cars, lorries and buses passing the school gates at set times of the day and can collate the results to present them mathematically. However, when you think about it, if you did the same thing, you would have to take other things into account before you, at a higher level, could come to any valid conclusions regarding the density of traffic outside the school and the need or otherwise to move a bus stop or provide a school crossing. Research 'proper' is not so simple.

Whatever form your assignment takes, you will still need to edit what you have done. If you take your work seriously, you will have made more than one draft and will have probably had to rewrite some sections more than once.

Check your work first for content. Have you used the

correct terminology? Are your facts and statements correct and well supported by evidence? Does what you say make sense, not just to you, but to anyone else who may read it?

Check your language use. Are your sentences sensible, nicely balanced in length and easy to read? Have you paragraphed as you should? (Have you paragraphed at all?)

Check that quotations are in quotation marks and referenced. Check spellings. If you know that you are a poor speller pay particular attention to this. As you can use a dictionary and references at this point there is no excuse for incorrect spellings. Many very intelligent people have been poor at spelling, but knowing that this was so, they have acknowledged the problem and have done something about it.

Are all diagrams, maps and illustrations clearly labelled?

Finally, put your work together in a clearly designated order. Write a contents page if appropriate and a bibliography if you have used other material and acknowledge any quotations and references that you may have used in your work.

That's it. For those of you who enjoy presentation, attractive covers, binders and so on, add to the pleasure of your achievement, and also give pleasure to the person whose job it is to assess what you have done.

To sum up

1. Assignments can take several forms. Ensure that you know what is involved in your particular course and also how you will be assessed.
2. Learn to recognise the different purposes of your assignments so that you present them in an appropriate format.
3. Reports deal with factual information and should be presented as accurately as possible. Use different kinds

of presentation to make your intentions clear.

4. Learn to structure 'project' type assignments so that they are informative, meaningful and, hopefully, enjoyable.

5. Be very aware of the potential pitfalls of 'Research'. Avoid making unsupported claims or statements. Check your 'evidence' with care.

6. Always give credit when you have used work done by others. Reference possible credits as you go along so that you know where they belong.

7. Edit your work carefully before handing it in.

8

MINDING YOUR LANGUAGE

English will not be the first language of many of the readers of this book. Because of this, I felt that a chapter on the use of English would be helpful. Such a chapter may also help those of you who have not had the benefit of formal English language teaching previously and who doubt your own ability to use English correctly.

Explanations of the uses of punctuation marks, confusing word meanings and spellings and some grammatical uses, it is hoped, will be of use to many of you. The task of explaining, in full, the complexities of the English language is another matter and will not be attempted here. It is an immense subject and any attempt to do more than has been suggested above would only end in confusion. However, it is not difficult to list and explain common errors in spellings and usage. Many years of correcting and marking students' work have shown me what these errors are likely to be.

Before looking at the most common errors in detail we need to say a little more about using language in general terms.

'Use your dictionary', you will frequently be told. Indeed, but sometimes the explanation you find only serves to confuse you further. The explanation itself may refer you to other words which are equally unknown to you. This kind of experience does not give you confidence. Often, the dictionary will refer to another language from which the word derives and you are expected to understand.

Very often, understanding why you find something difficult to deal with can help to give you confidence to solve the problem. A brief explanation of how the English language has evolved over time may help to make its usage more clear. It is useful to be aware that English has assimilated many other languages over time to become the language that we use now. Assimilations, inclusions and additions have occurred because of invasions of the British Isles by peoples such as the Romans (Latin), the Anglo-Saxons (Germanic languages), the Vikings (Scandinavian languages of Norway, Sweden and Denmark), and finally the Normans (French). Later, Britain's world role resulted in additions from other languages such as Arabic and Indian. Many English words also derive from Greek, particularly in mathematics and the sciences.

Today, English is spoken world-wide, it is said, by approximately 750 million people. In its many forms, 'English', 'American English', 'Australian English' and so on, it is the first or second language of many, and a language of communication for those for whom it is the only language they share with other foreigners.

Naturally then, English is not a rigid language, but one which is constantly evolving and changing with use. You will find differences in spellings between American English and English. Don't worry about this too much. Just be aware of the differences and find out which version your school, college or university prefers you to use in your work.

An awareness of the mixture of languages that is English will maybe help those of you who find the seeming lack of rules confusing. Classical scholars perhaps have an advantage over the most of us. They are comfortable with the understanding that the plural form of memorandum is memoranda, a crisis becomes many crises; a phenomenon, phenomena; formula, formulae; radius, radii, and so on. (Find out what the plural of 'index' would be.)

The rule of the use of ie/ei

Take the rule of the use in spelling of ie or ei. Which comes first and when? The 'rule' says 'I before E except after C'. Except sometimes. When? The following spellings are correct: niece, piece, ceiling, deceive. They follow the rule. However, these words are also correct: beige, foreign, height, and they do not follow the rule. A dictionary will certainly be of use to you in this case.

Common language problems

Only a specialist in grammar (a grammarian) could claim to write in a language without any mistakes. Very few of us could say that we have never made a mistake. However, many of the more common mistakes made in written work can be easily avoided if correct use is noted and learned.

Words which students need to be aware of are those which sound the same when spoken but which are spelt differently and have very different meanings. Very often, there is confusion about these simple words because of the way in which they are pronounced and used by others. We all speak in a slack and lazy way at times and that does not help our spelling. The following words are those which are most often misused:

To (preposition/part of infinitive verb), **Too** (as well as) and **Two** (number 2)

There (place), **They're** (they are) and **Their** (belonging to them)

Who (that person), **Whose** (belonging to that person), and **Who's** (who is)
('**Who**' and '**How**' are often confused)
Know (knowledge) and **No** (negative)
Where (place) and **Wear** (clothes, wear out)
Brought (to bring) and **Bought** (to buy)
Were (in the past) and **We're** (we are)
Caught (to catch) and **Court** (where legal cases are heard)
Fought (battled) and **Fort** (a fortification)

There are other words which are spelt in a similar way but which are pronounced differently and which mean different things. For example we have:

Our (sounds '*owr*') and **Are** (sounds '*arr*')

An effort made to differentiate between the above and similar words in spelling and in meaning will be valuable in all work in English.

Other frequently experienced errors are to do with several simple expressions which can easily be corrected with a little attention and effort.

Different from/Similar to
In English it is correct to say 'different from' and 'similar to'. Think of 'difference' as a pushing apart and away from and 'similarity' as movement towards and you will get this right.

Less/Fewer
It is correct to use the term 'fewer' when referring to a

number of things made smaller in number and 'less' when referring to a whole thing made smaller. Think of there being 'less' cake after some has been eaten, and 'fewer' sweets when some have been eaten.

Imply/Infer

To 'imply' means to suggest something. An 'implication' is something suggested, if not actually clearly stated. To 'infer', on the other hand, means to gather that something is meant even if it is not actually said. So we 'infer' from something that is 'implied', as in 'He inferred from what she implied that he was not to be promoted'.

Comprise

Take care with the word 'comprise'. Comprise contains 'of' within itself and does not need another 'of'. ('Comprised of' means 'made up of of', which is nonsense.)

Effect/Affect

Even though the words 'effect' and 'affect' have different meanings as well as different spellings, they are frequently wrongly used as substitutes for each other. An 'effect' is a noun, it is the result of something that happens. To 'affect' is a verb, and means 'to act upon' or 'to influence'. These two words do look and sound very much alike but they are not the same. Correct use of each would be for example: 'The climate *affects* her health badly' (Verb). 'The climate has a bad *effect* on her health' (Noun).To 'take effect' means to begin to work, to become operative, to have a result, as in: 'The changes will *take effect* as from next Monday', or 'The changes will be *effective* from next Monday'. These changes may of course 'affect' someone adversely (badly) when they become 'effective'.

Proscribe/Prescribe

'Prescribe' means to recommend or direct. Think of a prescription written by a doctor which recommends a particular medicine to a patient. A prescription 'prescribes' what medicine or treatment the patient should take. Doctors may also prescribe a rest or time off work. You can get a prescription for glasses.

To 'proscribe' is quite different. It originates, possibly, from the Roman custom of 'proscribing' a person by putting up a poster declaring them to be an outlaw. So to 'proscribe' something or someone is to make it or them forbidden, banished, condemned in some way, prohibited or ostracised. Unpleasant indeed . . .

Wander/Wonder

Wander and wonder sound almost the same when spoken, although they shouldn't if pronounced properly. Their meanings are quite different, however. To 'wander', which is a verb, means to move about without any decided direction, as in: 'He wandered about all over the place'. To 'wonder', which is also a verb, means to think questioningly about something, as in: 'I wonder what we will find in the box?'

Stationery/Stationary

These two words do sound the same but their different endings give different meanings. 'Stationary' means not moving, remaining in the same place, being still, as in: 'The car was stationary in the traffic jam', which means that the car was not moving.

'Stationery', on the other hand, means writing materials, such as paper, pens, ink, envelopes, rulers and so on. 'We bought stationery at the stationers so that we could write our letters.'

Compliment/Complement

A 'compliment' is a word or action which shows admiration or respect for something that is said or done. One is normally said to 'pay' or be 'paid' a compliment, as in: 'She was paid a compliment about her new hair style', or 'It was a compliment to be asked to open the fête'. 'Compliment' can also be used as a verb as in: 'I compliment you on your success'.

'Complement' is something (a person or thing) that makes something else complete, as in: 'That hat will complement the outfit perfectly', or 'The ship has a full complement of men'.

In mathematics (Geometry) 'complementary' is the name given to an angle which when added to another gives 90° (a Right angle).

Neither/Nor, Either/Or

These words complement each other when they are used in a sentence together. As in: 'They were neither happy nor sad'. As in 'Either you will, or you won't', meaning 'this' or 'that', or 'this one' or 'that one'.

Small/Little

The difference between these becomes quite clear when you realise that you can make something 'smaller' but you cannot make something 'littler'. It is possible to have a 'small' amount but little is the only word which will stand alone. As in: 'Thank you, I will have a little' (of whatever it is), but not 'I will have a small'. A 'small' what?

Quite/Quiet

These two words do not sound the same. When they are used in place of each other it is because the writer has been careless with spelling. 'Quite', either meaning 'to the greatest extent', or 'somewhat', and 'quiet' meaning little or no sound, are obviously different in meaning. 'Quite' can be used in many ways, 'quiet' cannot.

During/For

'During' is used when referring to a period of time, to something happening within a time limit. As in: 'It happened during the afternoon' or 'During World War Two many lives were lost'.

'For', on the other hand, although also used with reference to time as in: 'He slept for an hour', has many other uses, as in: 'He went for a walk' and 'For instance'.

I/Me

We think of 'I' as the subject and 'me' as the object of a sentence. Often when people are struggling to speak or write correctly, they replace 'me' with 'I' quite unnecessarily. They do this because they assume, quite incorrectly, that it is more polite to do so. Correct use is quite simple if you follow these guidelines. If for example, you say: 'My husband and I', and mean something like 'My husband and I think highly of the cook', you are quite correct because you are saying 'My husband thinks highly of the cook and I think highly of the cook'. However, you cannot properly say 'It was given to my husband and I' as you would not say 'It was given to I'. Rather you would say, correctly, 'It was given to me'. 'It was given to my husband and it was also given to me', so 'It was given to my husband and me'.

Minute/Minute

Two small words spelt in exactly the same way, pronounced quite differently and with quite distinct meanings. 'Minute' (pronounced 'minnit') means a period of time or a note of a meeting, and 'Minute' (pronounced 'mynute') means very small indeed.

Whether/Weather

Pronounced exactly the same (unless a perfectionist chooses to sound the 'wh' as in 'why', 'where' and 'when'). 'Whether', used as a 'conjunction' (a word joining one group of words to another), to show consideration of choice, as in: 'One did not know whether to stay or go', or sometimes used instead of 'either'. 'Weather' is the day to day expression of climate i.e. rain, sunshine, wind, snow.

Accent and dialect

There is sometimes confusion between these two. 'Accent' refers to the way in which words are pronounced, how they sound when spoken. 'Dialect' refers to a particular way of using language in a particular part of the country. People from the North and South of England pronounce words differently and sometimes have different words for the same things. So is it in other parts of the United Kingdom, in Wales and Scotland for example. Accent and dialect add 'colour' and interest to a language and are not to be feared. However, the form of English emphasised in this book is that which has universally been understood as 'Standard English', generally considered to be the most 'correct' and easily understood form in both writing and speech. It might be said to be the most 'transferable' for learning and study.

Etcetera

Finally, beware of the use of etcetera. 'Etc.' so often gives the impression that although there is more to be said the writer cannot be bothered to say it. In effect it says 'There is a lot more to this but you must work that out yourself'.

Punctuation, full stops and commas

Try reading a passage aloud without acknowledging any punctuation marks and without pausing for breath. Your reading will be boring and almost meaningless. It will be difficult for a listener to understand what you are saying. Then read the same passage with punctuation included. Pause for commas and pause longer at full stops. Acknowledge speech, exclamation and question marks by the tone of your voice. Your reading will now be meaningful.

Commas, full stops, paragraphs and other marks are needed for sense and meaning. Without punctuation, spoken or written words cannot be properly arranged and understood. Full stops are needed to vary the length of sentences. Normally we use a full stop when a sentence is complete in itself. However, a lot of short sentences, one after the other, do not make the reader or listener feel comfortable. It is better to vary the length of sentences in written and spoken language. For this, we need commas. A comma is like a short intake of breath, a short pause before continuing.

Question marks and exclamation marks

Question marks are used to end a sentence which is also a question. Question marks contain their own full stops so that there is no need to add another. Exclamation marks also contain their own full stops. These are useful to emphasise what has been said. They draw attention to an amusing statement or show that what has been said is felt very strongly. (Fancy that! Well!) Please do not use exclamation marks too often though, as over use will destroy their effect. It is rather like shouting. Shout all the time and eventually no one will listen. Raise your voice only rarely and others will immediately notice and will pay attention to what you say.

Apostrophes

Many people report difficulty using apostrophes correctly. The first thing to remember is that there are only two kinds of apostrophe. One is the apostrophe of omission. The other is the apostrophe of possession. Omission has to do with leaving out. Possession is to do with ownership. The apostrophe of omission is used when a letter has been left out of a word or letters have been left out of a group of words. The most common omissions are ones we use in speech all the time without thinking about them. Words such as 'don't' (do not), 'won't' (will not), 'can't' (can not), 'shan't' (shall not), 'couldn't' (could not), 'wouldn't' (would not), 'shouldn't' (should not), 'it's' (it is), 'he's' (he is), 'she's' (she is), 'haven't' (have not), 'they're' (they are), 'we're' (we are), and 'you're' (you are).

The possessive apostrophe is used when something belongs to someone or something else. We add an apostrophe 's' to show possession, e.g. The boy's sister, teacher's book, mother's shoes and father's slippers. In these cases there is one boy, one teacher, one mother and one father. We make the sister, book, shoes and slippers belong to them by adding an apostrophe 's'. Here we are dealing with single things, that is, singular nouns. When we deal with plural nouns, we can still use the apostrophe to show possession but we use it slightly differently, like this: we turn 'boy' singular into 'boys' plural by adding an 's'. Then we add the apostrophe afterwards to show possession. That is, 'we saw the boys' sister'. Similarly we add an 's' then the apostrophe to teachers' (plural), mothers' (plural) and fathers' (plural). We say then: The teachers' book (many teachers), The mothers' shoes (several mothers) and The fathers' slippers (more than one father). We can then say for example: 'The cat's kittens' (one cat and her kittens) and 'The cats' kittens' (many cats and their kittens – there are still a lot of kittens!). There are some plural nouns which do not end in 's': words like 'women' and 'men' and 'gentlemen'. These words use the possessive apostrophe 's' in the normal way, e.g. women's hats and men's coats.

Take care with the little word 'it'. Remember 'it's' means 'it is', using the apostrophe of omission. 'Its', when used as a possessive, does not need an apostrophe. If you think about it, we do not need a possessive apostrophe with words which are possessive in themselves, words such as their (belonging to them), your (belonging to you), her (belonging to her), his (belonging to him), our (belonging to us). So, we do not need one with 'its' (belonging to it). There are many people today who will use an apostrophe every time a word ends in 's'. It makes no sense. Incorrect use can be seen all around us, on shop fronts, advertisement boards, and, even worse, in students' work!

Speech marks, quotation marks and inverted commas
The marks above are used in three ways: one, to indicate speech, that is, words which are actually said; two, to indicate a title of a poem, essay or other short piece of writing

(N.B. titles of books, plays etc. should be <u>underlined</u> or *italicised*); and three, to acknowledge a quotation, that is, words which have been taken from some other writing.

To understand the correct use of 'speech' marks, think of cartoon or comic characters and their speech 'bubbles'. All the words in the 'bubbles' are words which the speaker actually says and should be within the marks. The rule is really quite simple. The marks enclose the words said. This means that they are used before the speech begins and after it ends. At the beginning of speech, it is correct to use a capital letter as we would to begin a sentence. Speech ends with a full stop, question mark or an exclamation mark, and the speech marks themselves then 'close' the speech. If the speaker begins, pauses and then continues speaking within the same sentence, a capital letter is not needed for the continuation of the speech. Like this:

Mary said, 'Hello John, how are you?'
'Hello John', Mary said, 'how are you?'

Note the use of a comma *after* the word 'said'. Remember also that each new speaker must be separated from the previous speaker. Begin a new speaker on a different line. If this is not done it will not be clear who is saying what. Practise will help. Try some simple exercises at this point if you feel you need to do so.

There is a difference between what is called 'direct', speech which we have just examined, and what is called 'reported' speech. 'Direct' speech, as we have seen, is the words actually said. 'Reported' speech on the other hand is what someone *says* someone else has said. Like this: Mary asked John how he was. John said that he was well. If we turn John's speech into direct speech, it will look like this: John said, 'I am well'. To use a quotation within a quotation or speech within a speech, use double marks for one and single marks for the other, like this: John said, 'He said, "Go away"', so I did'.

To use quotation marks or inverted commas to indicate titles or quotations, we simply put them around the words we wish to emphasise. Like this: 'The Lady of Shallot' by Alfred Lord Tennyson, for titles, and for quotations, 'To be or not to be', as Hamlet said.

Other punctuation marks which are used less often are those known as colons (:) and semi-colons (;). They are used much more rarely, because most of the time we can manage without them. Using just full stops and commas can be enough for most of the writing we do until we are working at a higher level. Also, of course, many people have no idea how they can be used and don't know what to do with them.

Briefly, a colon can be used to introduce a list of things, can be used before an explanation, an example of what is being talked about, or a long quotation. A semi-colon is a pause in writing which is longer than a comma but not as long as a full stop. It can also be used to separate two parts of a sentence which are very close together in meaning. If you are comfortable with these two marks, then use them by all means. If you are not, do not worry; they are not essential to your work.

Other punctuation marks used are called hyphens, dashes and brackets. All of these have their uses but all need to be used with care. Brackets are very useful for helping to make things more clear, by giving an alternative to what has been said, or making an aside. Dashes are simply used to separate words or groups of words when necessary. Overuse of such marks however is not a good idea as it can give the impression of carelessness.

As was said previously, a student who is unsure of the uses of the more complex punctuation marks would be well-advised to concentrate on the correct use of more simple forms. Don't worry too much about colons, semi-colons and complicated plural possessives. Concentrate on the correct use of full stops, commas, exclamation marks (sparingly), question marks and simple apostrophes of omission and possession. Learn how to use speech marks correctly if you need to use them. Understand the difference between direct and reported speech. Stay simple.

What has been said does not cover all aspects of language use by any means. It does, however, as far as possible, refer to the kinds of mistake most commonly found in students' work and, hopefully, will be of help in avoiding unnecessary misuse of language.

To sum up

1. It helps to be aware that the English language has evolved over time from the amalgamation of many other languages.
2. Careless pronunciation can lead to careless and/or incorrect spelling as often words which *do* sound the same have different spellings and meanings.
3. Grammatical errors are common, but the correct forms can be learned.
4. Accent and dialect are not the same.
5. Punctuation is necessary for the sense of what we write.
6. Do not over use exclamation marks and question marks.
7. There are two kinds of apostrophe, (i) possession and (ii) omission.
8. Use speech marks for words actually said. Begin each person's speech on a separate line.
9. Use quotation marks for direct speech, quotation and titles of poems, essays and articles. Underline or italicise titles of books, plays, films and so on.

10. Use hyphens, dashes and brackets appropriately or not at all.
11. Do not worry about more complex punctuation marks if you are unsure about them.
12. Practise if you need to do so.

9

UNDERSTANDING TERMS
USED IN LANGUAGE

When using language, whether written or spoken, we obey certain rules, even if we do not know what they are. In Chapter 6, and in references to the use of punctuation, you were advised to 'keep things simple'. Books about grammar will tell you what a 'simple' sentence (or any sentence for that matter) should contain. That is, a subject, a verb and an object arranged in a certain way to make sense.

All this really means is that a sentence should say who is doing what and to whom. More complex sentences will say how and why, and when and where. It can be great fun learning to analyse such sentences, learning to recognise how groups of words fit into particular 'parts of speech' and what those 'parts of speech' are called. We can usefully look at some of the words we could encounter, see what they mean and how we should understand them. Remember, language is a tool for us to use, to explain, to communicate and learn with. The more easily we can use language, the more we can say, the better we will be understood and, therefore, the more effective we will be. Ideas are all very well but we need to be able to express them.

Most of you will know what vowels and consonants are. For those of you who are unsure (because perhaps you have never been told and did not like to ask!), they are names given to letters of the English alphabet. Five letters are vowels: A, E, I, O and U. The remainder are consonants except for 'Y' which is sometimes thought of and used as a vowel.

We do need to know the difference between vowels and consonants because sometimes they are referred to when rules of spelling are being explained. Small children are taught the rule of the 'MAGIC E', to explain how adding an 'e' to the end of the word changes the sound of the vowel within the word, as in: bad, bade; fad, fade; not, note and so on.

More terminology

Nouns
A noun is a word which stands for a person, place or thing. Nouns can be 'proper', 'common', 'abstract' or 'collective'. They can also be 'compound'.
A 'proper' noun is the name of a particular person or a particular place, e.g. London, Mrs. Jones, Mr. Jones.
A 'common' noun is a person, place or thing which does not have a special name, e.g. city, woman, man.
An 'abstract' noun is an 'idea', a word which means something that is not concrete, something which cannot be touched, e.g. happiness, misery, hope.
A 'collective' noun refers to a group of people or things, e.g. couple (Mr. and Mrs. Jones), crowd (a number of people).
'Compound' nouns are words which are made up of two other nouns to make another word, e.g. sales + man = salesman, book + maker = bookmaker.

Pronouns
These are exactly what they say they are, words which stand

'for' (pro) nouns. When we speak or write, we do not wish to repeat the name of a person or place each time we refer to that person or place, so we use a *pro*-noun instead. E.g. City – it, Happiness – it, Mrs. Jones – she, Mr. Jones – he, Woman – she, Man – he, Couple – they (meaning two people). Some collective nouns will take a singular pronoun when used to mean a single thing. We need not be too pedantic about this as long as we know what we mean and our readers and listeners can understand our meaning.

Gender
When a pronoun is used, you will notice that it indicates GENDER. Gender distinguishes between the male and female of something. If something is neither male nor female, or we do not know what it is, it is referred to as a 'neuter', an 'it'.

In English, the male/masculine is 'he', plural 'they'. The female/feminine 'she' is also plural 'they'. For animals of unknown gender we use 'it', and again the plural 'they'. Most things are also 'it'. However, you will find that some 'things' are often *given* gender and referred to as if they are female or feminine. This can be the case with ships, cars and countries. For example, one's own country is often referred to as the 'Motherland'. France is frequently referred to as 'she' and even sometimes, as 'Marianne'. We hear people speak of 'Mother India', and 'Mother Russia'. An exception is when reference is made to Germany, which is referred to as the 'Fatherland'. Why this should be so is left to you to consider. Historians among you may have some ideas about it.

Words which refer to male and female people will be given masculine or feminine form, such as: man – woman, boy – girl, nephew – niece, son – daughter, brother – sister, husband – wife, uncle – aunt, granddad – grandma, sir –

madam. However, if the gender is not known we can say person, baby, child, relation, sibling, teenager, grandparent, friend and so on instead.

Words which refer to rank also denote gender such as: King – Queen, Prince – Princess, Duke – Duchess, Earl – Countess, Lord – Lady, Marquis – Marchioness. With occupational nouns which could be of either sex such as doctor, teacher, student, lecturer, surgeon, we need to state whether the person is male or female. That is, if it matters whether or not we know! Exceptions to this are words such as: waiter – waitress, host – hostess, hero – heroine, which denote gender in themselves. Today, it is increasingly common to substitute 'person' for words which would previously have indicated gender, such as 'salesperson' and 'chairperson' instead of salesman/woman or chairman/woman.

Gender also applies to the animal world, when we refer to the male or the female of a species, as in: Tiger – tigress, lion – lioness, duck – drake, boar – sow, buck – doe, gander – goose. Notice that the female/feminine gender is not always shown by the addition of 'ess' to the masculine form.

Plurals

Most plurals in English are formed by adding 's' to the singular form of the word. E.g. coat – coats, hat – hats, cat – cats. Some though, end in 'es' as in potatoes or tomatoes. This depends on the original (singular) word ending. For words which end in 'o' add 'es'. For words which end in 'sh', 'ss' and 'x', add 'es'. As in: bush – bushes, cross – crosses, mix – mixes.

There are exceptions (as always) which need to be noted, e.g. piano becomes pianos when just an 's' is added to the word ending in 'o'. This rule applies normally to words of foreign origin, e.g. kimonos. For words which end in 'y', we usually remove the 'y' and add 'ies'. As in: puppy – puppies, lolly – lollies, baby – babies. BUT, for words which end in 'y' after a *vowel*, we only add an 's'. E.g. key – keys, ray – rays. Following the usual 'rule' would result in some odd words!

Much confusion is caused by the few nouns ending in 'f' or 'fe'. What we do here is remove the 'f' or 'fe' and add 'ves'. There are twelve words which we must treat like this and they are all listed here: wife – wives, knife – knives, self – selves, leaf – leaves, wolf – wolves, thief – thieves, shelf – shelves, sheaf – sheaves, half – halves, calf – calves, loaf – loaves, life – lives. Some 'f' words can take either 's' or 'ves' as you wish. You *cannot* say 'wifes' or 'knifes' and be correct, but you can say 'scarfs' or 'scarves', 'dwarfs' or 'dwarves'.

Even more about plural nouns
Sometimes, some nouns change their vowels when they change from singular to plural. E.g. foot – feet, tooth – teeth, mouse – mice, louse – lice, woman – women, child – children.

Look for other 'collective' nouns, such as a 'pride' of lions, a 'flock' of sheep, a 'gaggle' of geese, a 'troop' of monkeys. Such nouns are usually treated as singular nouns and therefore take a singular pronoun. E.g. 'The pride (it) hunts', 'Our team (it) won'. *But* 'The team (they) wore red shirts', because the shirts are worn by the separate team members. The meaning of the word will determine whether it should be seen as singular or plural. Check words such as 'police', 'scissors' and 'stairs' which are used as plurals. There are others. Remember that, as we have seen already, words derived from Latin or Greek use the rules of these languages to form their plurals.

Articles

You will hear reference to 'definite' and 'indefinite' articles. They are very easy to understand. A definite article 'the' refers to a particular specific object or thing. E.g. 'The oasis was a welcome sight' and 'The dog's name was Bill'.

An indefinite article on the other hand refers to an object or thing but to no particular one. E.g. 'I would like to have a dog', 'An oasis is found in a desert'.

Adjectives

Adjectives are words which tell us more about nouns. That is, they give us more information about a person or thing. Using adjectives gives colour, shape and interest to what we say or write. Adjectives can be said to 'describe' nouns. They are the same when used in the singular or plural form. E.g. the red dress, the red dresses. BUT (there is always a but!), we say: this – the one here (singular), that – the one there (singular), these – the ones here (plural), those – the ones there (plural).

When using adjectives, we can also use them as 'comparatives' and 'superlatives': For example, we can say that something is 'good', 'better' or 'best'. The correct use of comparatives and superlatives can be checked by reference to a dictionary. They do not always follow the 'er', 'est' rule. For example look at: little, less, least; much, many, more, most. With adjectives which could become 'clumsy' and difficult to pronounce, by adding 'er' or 'est', it is usual to use 'more' and 'most' before the word to make a comparison or superlative. For example, we would say 'More intelligent' and 'Most intelligent', not, as some small children might say, 'intelligentest'. Young children are actually showing language awareness when they do this.

Learning experience leads to more 'correct' language use for all of us. We also make use of 'as' and 'than' when comparing one thing with another. As in: 'Your marks were as good as mine' and 'Your marks were better than mine'.

Verbs

Verbs, we are taught, are 'doing' words, they refer to action, to movement. We 'write', 'run', 'jump', 'learn', 'study', 'hope' and so on. When using verbs we need to take care to use the correct tense. We must make it clear whether the action we are talking about is taking place now (present), has taken place (past), or will take place (the future). There are other more complicated explanations of tenses than this. We use them quite naturally in speech all the time, normally being unaware that we are doing so. We know much more and are much more clever than we realise!

In English, we do not have to worry about matching verbs with the gender of our subject, only to be aware whether it is singular or plural. We have in English, as in French, for example, first, second and third persons singular, and first, second and third persons plural, as in I, you, he/she, it, we, you (pl), they.

However, 'you' refers to both the singular and plural persons and carries the same form of verb, unlike French where the singular *tu* and plural *vous* carry different verb endings and also refer to the informal and formal forms of address. Those of you who are students of English literature may encounter the archaic forms of 'you' singular, such as 'thee', and 'thou'.

The student working in English does not have to worry about making verb endings 'agree' in spite of all the 'BUTS' so far.

Adverbs

As adjectives tell us more about nouns, so do adverbs tell us more about verbs. Using adverbs enables us to describe actions in greater detail and makes our speech and writing more interesting.

Most adverbs are formed by adding 'ly' to the word used to describe our action, e.g. quiet – quietly. Not all, however (another BUT). There are exceptions to this rule and these can be learned. As with comparatives and superlatives, the construction of adverbs from other words relates to the clumsiness, or otherwise, of the spoken word. Examples: 'true' becomes 'truly' (the 'e' is removed and 'ly' added), 'pretty' becomes 'prettily' and 'happy becomes 'happily' (remove the 'y', change it to 'i' and add 'ly'.

We refer to adverbs of manner, place, time and frequency, and all that means is we use words to say how, where, when and how often something happens or is done.

Conjunctions

Don't let this word worry you. A conjunction is just one of the words we use all the time to join our sentences together. Rather like cement between building bricks is used to make a wall, such words are used to 'fill in' the spaces and work to make the sentences 'make sense'. They are simple words and we use them usually without realising we are doing so. Examples are: 'but', 'and', 'so', 'still', 'yet', 'though', 'for', 'because', 'either – or', 'neither – nor', 'however', 'otherwise' and 'also'. Very useful they are too.

To sum up

1. Do not be afraid of language, it is for us to use.
2. Nouns are the names of places, people or things.
3. Pronouns 'stand in' for nouns.
4. Gender tells you whether something or someone is male/masculine or female/feminine.

5. Most plurals end in 's'. For those that do not, see the 'rules'.
6. A definite article refers to a specific thing, e.g. 'the'. An indefinite article refers to something, but not specifically, e.g. 'a', 'an'.
7. Adjectives tell us more about nouns.
8. Verbs denote action. Adverbs tell us *how* something is done.
9. Conjunctions join words together to make sensible sentences.

10
ANALYSING ESSAY TITLES

The method of analysis recommended and shown here is a very simple one. Concise and straight to the point, this approach uses the words and phrases in the title itself and puts them into numbered order to make the essay structure (the ingredients of our 'cake'). The instructions, which tell us what to do (the verb in the title), are our 'method'. The numbered items are the content (ingredients) in the order which they should or could be added to our 'recipe' or 'essay'.

If you are tense and nervous in a test or examination situation, question analysis gives you something to 'do', helps you to begin to write and means that, when you do begin, you will write about the question. This should help you until you settle down and become more sure about what you are doing. The technique is useful too for coursework essays and questions as, again, it will help you to get started when inspiration is lacking and a deadline is in sight.

Essay questions are more likely to be found in some subjects than others. They are also more likely to be found at a higher level. Whatever the question, however, whether a conventional essay, shorter format essay or a question divided into parts, analysis will still usefully apply.

Analysis
The following history questions have been taken from a

paper that has been worked by pupils preparing for 'A' level examinations. Conventional essay answers were expected.

Example 1 (History)
' "The U.N. was formed, not to lead us to Heaven, but to save us from Hell" (Dag Hammarskjöld).

Using examples from the 1990s, analyse the success and failure of U.N. peace-keeping operations in the light of this statement.'

You may not be an historian and, even if you are, you may not be familiar with the subject area, but you can analyse the question. How? What are you told to do? Method: *analyse*. What are you to 'analyse'? 'The success and failure of U.N. peace-keeping operations in the light of this statement'. What statement? Dag Hammarskjöld's statement. How? By 'using examples from the 1990s'. So, recipe ingredients are as follows:

1. The U.N. *(what?)*
2. Dag Hammarskjöld *(who?)* intro
3. Was formed *(Why? When?)*
   (a) not to lead us to Heaven, but
   (b) to save us from hell.
4. Examples from the 1990s peace-keeping oper-ations.
5. Successes? *(analyse – cook)*
6. Failures? *(analyse – cook)*
7. Conclude – refer back to 1 and 3a and b *(serve)*

Your title analysis would look like this:

¹ [1]   ² [2]   ^{3(a)} [3(a)]

'{The U.N.} {was formed,} {not to lead us to Heaven,}

{but to save us from Hell'} {(Dag Hammarskjöld).}$^{3(b)}$ ^{2}
{Using examples^{4} from the 1990s,} {analyse^{7}} {the success^{5}} {and failure^{6}} {of U.N. peace-keeping operations^{4}} {in the light of this statement}'

Let us analyse another title, the other way round. This is the way you would need to approach a question under examination conditions, if you decide to use this method of analysis that is.

Example 2 (History)
'{Discuss^{7}} {the effects of^{6}} {the increasing globalisation of^{2}} {the world economy^{1}} on the {opposing forces^{5}} of {protectionism^{3}} and {free trade^{4}}.'

1. The world economy *(what is the subject?)*
2. Increasing globalisation *(what does this mean?)*
3. Protectionism *(what is this?)*
4. Free trade *(what is this?)*
5. (As) 3 + 4 opposing forces *(how? why?)*
6. The effects of 2 and 1 on 3 and 4.
7. Discuss 6 *(Method)*

The title gave you your answer. You were told that there is 'increasing globalisation of world economy'. You were told that protectionism and free trade are 'opposing forces'. You were told that one affects the other and asked to 'discuss' the effects of one on the other. What more could you need? Your answer is in the question.

Certainly, you could begin to write immediately by beginning with 'The effects of increasing globalisation of the world economy on . . .' and go on from there. But how could you go on? Where do you begin to discuss and what?

The analytical method shown gives you a structure from which to develop your answer. Points 1-7 in this example do not need to be of the same length but they do all need some mention because they are what the question is 'about'.

This pattern ensures that you miss nothing and you include everything. The actual 'answer' must reflect what you have been asked to do, in this case to 'Discuss'.

Example 3 (History)
'Under Brezhnev, the U.S.S.R reached the zenith of its power influence in the world. In 1982 the international position of the U.S.S.R. was weaker in all respects than it had been in 1964. Can these two views be reconciled?'

This is a lovely long title to pull apart and put together again. It is not an easy question to answer so you would have to depend on the content for guidance. First, you consider what you have been asked to do, which is to answer the question about the two statements. 'Can "they" be reconciled?'

In order to do this you would need to analyse statement 1 and then statement 2 and *then* decide whether they 'can be reconciled'.
Like this:

1. USSR under Brezhnev
2. Power and influence in the world
3. Zenith? (of 2?)
4. International position in 1964
5. (weaker) in 1982
6. Compare 4 and 5
7. Reconcile 1, 2, 3, and 4, 5, 6.

Can you see how your essay structure becomes apparent when you analyse in this way? You are not likely to leave anything out that is important, nor will you waste time with irrelevancies. Some essay titles can be very long indeed. These do need very careful analysis, but the answer you need will be there, as long as you remember the *method* and do as you are asked.

Very short questions need a different approach. Short titles can be the most difficult to deal with unless you have a suitable technique. You cannot 'analyse' a single word or even two or three words, as we have been doing above. Instead, you must develop the essay content by expanding the word or words, so that you have material to work with. You may be the kind of student who can take such a title and immediately have brilliant ideas about what to do with it and how to do it.

If you cannot do this easily (most of us cannot, not at first) then you need to apply your technique, and rapidly too in some circumstances. Questions like this are frequently found on general papers which are designed to test your ability to 'think on your feet'. They also test your general knowledge, the knowledge you should have acquired by general reading, your interest in and awareness of the world around you.

When you first meet such questions they seem impossible to answer, but they are not.

Some examples of General Studies questions:

1. 'Discrimination is inevitable'. Discuss.
2. 'Is objectivity possible?'
3. 'What is the purpose of humour?'
4. 'Can science be ethical?'

Number 1 is a statement. In order to 'discuss' this statement you must examine the meaning of 'discrimination' and give examples of it. Only then can you 'discuss' whether it is inevitable or not. This title should *not* be a vehicle for your own particular political viewpoint. So you must be careful here. You may or may not believe in the inevitability of discrimination, but that is not what you are being asked. You therefore need to refer to discrimination in its many forms, before you can 'discuss'. As you will only have three levels of analysis, that is:

(i)   Discrimination (content)
(ii) is inevitable (content)
(iii) Discuss (method).

You must expand them yourself. The expansion and guidance is not in the question. Similarly with Q2, Q3 and Q4

2. 'Is objectivity possible?'
    (i)   objectivity?
    (ii) is it possible?

So much work to do yourself. First 'expand' objectivity then (ii) consider whether it is possible in the light of your expansion, otherwise you will have an answer which will stretch to about a paragraph and no more. If you are asked for 600 to 1000 words, for example, you will be many words short, and many marks short, too. Try questions 3 and 4 for yourself. Use a technique that you like for the expansion.

Example 1 (English)
'How does William Blake use structure and language to explore a range of human emotions and experience? Refer to at least two poems in your answer.'
    This question can be analysed in the suggested manner.

1. (How does Blake use) structure?
2. (How does Blake use) language?

3. (to explore a range of) human emotions
4. (to explore a range of human) experiences?
5. Apply 1, 2, 3, 4 to poem 1 and poem 2.

Example 2 (English)
'Structure and use of language are important features of poetry. Choose two or three poems from this selection* where you think they are particularly significant'.
*An anthology (collection of poems) issued to students.

Analysis:
1. Choose two or three poems.
2. Structure as an important feature of poetry.
3. Language as an important feature of poetry.
4. Where you think 2 and 3 are particularly significant in relation to 1.

Example 1 (Religious Studies)
'Believing in life after death makes a big difference to the way people live their lives. With reference to two or three world religions, explain how this belief affects the lifestyle of members of these religious communities.'

What are you asked to do? Refer and 'explain'. What? How a particular belief affects lifestyle. You would of course, choose the religions to include those which *do* believe in life after death. They must be *world* religions, so you would not choose to write about a minority 'cult'.

Analysis:
1. 'With reference to two or three world religions' (*decide and choose*).
2. 'This belief' which is believing in life after death (*in what way for each?*).

3. 'affects the lifestyle of members of those religious communities'.
4. 'makes a big difference to the way people live their lives'.
5. Explain how, with reference to 3 and 4.

(Note: 'affects the lifestyle' and 'makes a big difference to' are *not* the same in meaning. You could conclude by referring to the quotation here, saying in effect, 'Yes, it *does* make a big difference, see what has been said about the effects on lifestyle'.)

Example 2 (Religious Studies)
'Why is it important for a religious community to have a centre of worship? Comment on this statement with reference to two or three world religions.'

Analysis:
1. Religious community.
2. Centre of worship.
3. Two or three world religions.
4. 3 and 1 in relation to 1 'comment'.
5. 3 in relation to 2 'comment'.
6. Why is it important? Conclusion.

Example 1 (Geography)
'With reference to a large located river basin you have studied:
   (a) show how both physical and human factors can make the river basin difficult to manage.
   (b) using examples from this river basin, explain how some management strategies can themselves cause further problems.'

Analysis (a):
1. With reference to a large located river basin you have studied.
2. Physical factors (which) can make the river basin difficult to manage.
3. Human factors (which) can make the river basin difficult to manage.
4. Show how both 2 and 3 can make the river basin difficult to manage.

Analysis (b):
1. Using examples from this river basin.
2. Some management strategies.
3. Further problems.
4. Explain how 2 'can themselves' cause 3.

You would not necessarily need to rewrite every word from the title in your plan, as long as you knew what you were doing and knew you would be reminded to include important points by the notes you had made.

Example 2 (Geography)
(a) 'What are the main causes of deforestation in the world's tropical rain forests?'
(b) 'Using an ecosystem that you have studied, other than the tropical rain forest, describe how the activities of people can damage that ecosystem.'

Analysis (a):
1. Deforestation.
2. In the world's tropical rain forests.
3. What are the main causes of 1 and 2?

Depending on how many words you are allowed or how

much space you are given for (a) you would either write an essay response, which would entail full explanations of 1 and 2 and 3 as an explanation of 'causes', or you would give a list of 'causes' after showing the examiner that you know what is meant by 'deforestation' and what and where the world's tropical rain forests are.

Analysis (b):
  1. An ecosystem you have studied.
  2. The activities of people.
  3. Can damage that ecosystem.
  4. Using 1 'describe' how 2 and 3 relate.

(Note here, the ecosystem you choose must *not* be the same as in (a).)

The advice given here about question and/or title analysis is intended to help you to begin writing and give you the confidence to tackle any question you may meet because you *know* it can be done.

Students who do not develop a technique of any kind can give some surprising (and, initially, amusing) answers to questions. They have quite clearly been unable to cope.

Answers to avoid (these have been known!)
1. 'Do you agree?'
Student answer: 'Yes'.
2. 'Is objectivity possible?'
Student answer: 'No, I don't think so'.
3. 'What is the purpose of humour?'
Student answer: 'To make us laugh?'
4. 'Can science be ethical?'
Student answer' 'No', 'Yes', 'I don't know', 'I'm not really sure'.

We may find such answers amusing. In reality, they are

not at all funny. Such answers show how desperate the students must have been and how unprepared for what they were expected to do. The purpose of this chapter is to make sure that this does not happen to you.

Test questions for analysis

Religious Studies
'All religions have creation stories. What is their purpose? Explain your answer fully with reference to two or three religions you have studied'.

History
'Why did Hitler invade Russia in 1941?'

Geography
'Describe and explain the changes to the agricultural workforce between 1950 and 1990.'

Geography
'Explain the environmental advantages of not allowing fuel and mineral resources to be developed in wilderness areas such as Antarctica.'

General Studies
'The poor will always be with us. Comment on this statement.'
'Animals are intended to be subservient to man. Do you agree?'
'To be prejudiced is natural. Discuss.'

To sum up
1.   Title analysis gives structure to your work and is

applicable to titles of all kinds and all subjects.

2. This method of analysis is particularly helpful when nervous and working to time as it helps you to begin.

3. The title will give you your answer if you arrange the title content intelligently and use the 'verb' in the title to 'answer the question'.

4. Longer titles are often easier to analyse than short ones because the latter must be expanded first.

5. To expand a title, use other techniques as suggested.

6. If you do not expand a title your answer may be inadequate in both content and length.

7. Using the suggested techniques, you should be able to analyse any title, even if the subject is unfamiliar to you.

11
EXAMINATIONS

Preparation

The most important part of your examination preparation is the work you will have done for your course so far. Reading, learning, attending seminars, lectures and lessons, writing notes and essays, doing coursework and practical work. Now you need to be as practical and determined about your revision and your examination practice as you have been about your work so far.

Just as you have been encouraged throughout this book to take control of your own learning, so you need to learn how to control an examination situation as far as you are able to do so. It is the unseen and unknown nature of examinations which causes so much anxiety. So, although we cannot do anything about the 'unseen' element before examination day, we can certainly do a great deal to lessen our anxiety about the 'unknown'. As you develop greater control of the unknown, you will become more confident in your ability to deal with the unseen content of the paper you will eventually face.

An unfamiliar situation is stressful in itself so you need to become thoroughly familiar with the situations you will meet. You also need to be confident that you have revised as well as you can. If you do your best before the examination you will be better prepared to do your best when the day comes.

Let us begin with revision.

Revision

Some study books recommend that a student revise constantly throughout a course, setting time aside each week to go over what has been done that week, sorting out notes, rewriting and so on. Very disciplined indeed. Realistically, it is most unlikely that you have done this, at least not every week! It is also unlikely that you sort out your notes so regularly, rewriting and condensing. What a paragon of virtue you would be if you did. Perhaps you are?

If, however, you are like the rest of us, you will have found it better to deal with notes as you do them. If you have followed the advice in the chapter on note-taking and making, your notes should be ready for use when you decide to begin serious revision.

What to do. Timetable/Diary

First, as for study, make yourself a timetable for the period when you intend to begin revision. How long before your exams is up to you. Two months perhaps? It does depend on how much work you still have to do, but most institutions recognise the need for a period of 'free' study time at the end of a course.

How many subjects or topics do you need to revise? Divide your time into subject areas and the subject areas into topics. Now is the time to condense your notes. Doing this now will concentrate your mind and you will give yourself easy access to the memory 'joggers' you need just before the examination. You will have learned by now how best *you* can learn and your condensed notes should provide you with all you need to recall and to make necessary associations without re-reading texts constantly.

If you have worked consistently well, your essays and coursework papers will be very useful to you now. Re-read these, noting comments made about them, reconsidering what you said if you need to do so. Note where you did particularly well and ensure that you revise those areas thoroughly. This will give you assurance that an examination question in this area should be well within your competence. For areas in which you did not do quite so well, try to understand why and put matters right. You should then be able to deal with questions in those areas as well. It is quite likely that, as you have now matured in your study, areas previously seen as problematic no longer are, much to your surprise and comfort.

Be sensible, you cannot do everything. Remember what has been said about study techniques and apply them here. You cannot re-read all the texts you have used over a long period, so you must rely on your notes and other work. This is why work must be done properly in the first place.

Rehearse
We would not expect to present a play on stage without first having a rehearsal. Several rehearsals in fact. Neither would we expect a football team to take the field for a match without practice. Why then should we expect to be able to deal with an examination without practice? Taking an examination should not be a guessing game, rather it should be the end product of a period of controlled, deliberate rehearsal.

In practical terms, what does it entail? You, as the candidate, will be expected to go to a certain place at a certain time, prepared to demonstrate your knowledge and learning. Examiners will 'judge' your 'performance'. You will most likely be expected to answer a series of questions on a question paper, or, if the examination is a practical one, do practical work in a laboratory, workshop or studio. No doubt you will have a theory paper too. Music students will be expected to perform and will most likely have an 'aural' examination. Language students have an 'oral' and an 'aural'. At degree level you may be chosen for a 'viva'. A 'viva' is an oral examination which normally takes place after the written paper has been completed. All that you are expected to do should be practised beforehand in situations as much like the real one as possible. In order to do this, you will need to know exactly what will be expected of you. Ideally, you should be told, if not, you must ask.

Written examinations – preparation
It is most important to become familiar with the appearances of the papers you will be given. For this reason, you will need to get hold of as many past papers as you can. Compare papers of past years with each other. Are they all the same? Has the layout or format changed? Are they asking the candidate the same kinds of questions each year? Is there evidence that the examiners include up-to-date topics in the papers? If there is, this should alert you to the need to revise a topic which you may have studied as new and important. Does your tutor or teacher have a favourite or 'pet' topic and, most important, is he or she involved in setting the examination? If the answer to these questions is 'yes', then clearly you would be well-advised to revise that one particularly well.

Check the time allowed. Note whether any questions are compulsory. See whether the paper is divided into sections and, if so, what instructions are given for dealing with these sections. Do you have a choice of questions? How many out of how many? Are there multi-choice questions? Are the marks for sections or parts shown? Or do all questions carry equal marks? Note if some topics turn up most or all of the time, in one form or another. You now need to begin to rehearse in earnest.

Papers

The papers will have shown you how much time you will be able to allocate to each question during the examination. You now need to practise answering a question within this time limit. Begin with one question. Do not expect at this stage to stay within your time allowance.

When studying, use a clock or a timer. Be brutal with yourself. Choose your question, set your timer and begin. Within the time you allow yourself:

(1) read the question
(2) sort it out – what are you asked to 'do'?
(3) make a brief plan
(4) write your answer
(5) check time – conclude

Stop when your time is up. How did you do? Did you waste time? Where? Doing what? Dithering? Don't dither. Get on with it. Of course it will not be perfect, how can it be. Continue to practise with single questions in this way until you feel it would be possible to do more than one in a session. Gradually increase the number of questions you do until you arrive at the point where you can do a whole paper. You must be at this stage before the examination because you will be required to do the whole paper then. How long you will be writing depends on the time allowed, 3 hours, 2½ hours?

As you practise in this way, you will become familiar with the 'rubric' of the papers you use. Pay close attention to this. Perhaps all the papers you use are the same, perhaps not. Do not take anything for granted. Always read the instructions.

What possible instructions?
Many possible instructions. One of the most important is that which tells you to write your name, number and centre number in the appropriate place. Do not be anonymous!

Instructions from actual papers – the 'rubric'
Example 1: 'Paper one. Answer one question from this paper. Answers should be 600-800 words in length.'

'*Information for candidates*' will tell you where to write your name, number and centre number. It tells you that you *must* use the booklet given for your answers, but that you can also use supplementary sheets which you *must* attach to the booklet with your name and the question number you have done, clearly shown.

Example 2: Instructions. 'Answer *all* questions.' In '*Information for candidates*' this paper gives the number of marks possible for each question or part-question. Candidates are told that marks will be *given* for spelling, punctuation and grammar (not *deducted* for poor spelling, punctuation and grammar), that answers 'must be relevant and give full information for full marks' and 'Answers should always be supported by knowledge and understanding. Candidates are warned that 'unfair practice', that is, cheating, will mean no certificate will be given. The time allowance for this particular paper was ¾ hour out of a 1¾ hour examination. That is what it said, note, *not* 1¾ hour examination. Read carefully.

Example 3: Instructions for 1 hour of 1¾ hour exam.
'Answer Q1 (Section A)

Answer Q2 (Section B)

And EITHER Q3 OR Q4 (Section C).'

Information for candidates is the same as above.

In order to obey these instructions correctly you need to realise that Q1 *is* Section A and Q2 *is* Section B (it is a pity they did not say so!). The questions themselves remind the candidate to 'answer all parts of this question'. For example, Section A contains a picture as a source and questions on it, set out as (a)–(i), (ii), (iii), (iv), and (b) tells the candidate to choose *one* item from the source and answer *two* questions on it. The marks possible for both (a) and (b) are given. (c) also has two questions. (d) has one question which carries even more marks and requires an even more informative answer. Section B (Q2) is similar but is on a different topic. Section C gives the candidate two choices. 'Answer either Q3 or Q4'. Q3 gives a source C to use with questions (a) and (b) on it. Q4 gives a source D to use, also with questions (a) and (b) on it. Allocated marks are given for both.

Is it clear? Perhaps there should be an award for deciphering instructions!

The point is, you must make it clear to yourself, train yourself to do this and become so familiar with the kind of papers you will meet that you will not make silly mistakes. It is so easy to make silly mistakes when anxious, to answer too many questions or too few. What a waste of time and of marks. How dreadful too if you forget to put your name on your carefully worked supplementary sheets. How shocking if you do not number your answers!

Practical work

Those of you who need to incorporate practical work into your examination practice must do exactly that. You will no doubt be given opportunities to take 'mock' or 'trial' exams if you are at school and maybe you will also be allowed the use of workshops, studios and laboratories at a higher level. Whenever possible, extend your practical experience as much as you can. There is no substitute for the experience of working to time in examination conditions, therefore you need to create such conditions for yourself, as far as you are able to do so.

Timing is crucial and it is essential that you develop the ability to do your work within the time limitations expected. Practice is the only way. Do not be tempted to think it will be all right on the day because you know what you are doing. Yes, indeed you will know what you are doing, but if you do not have the time in which to do it, you will not be able to show the examiners that you do!

What do examiners want?
Contrary to popular opinion, examiners do not wish to fail you. They are not gleefully looking for your mistakes or for what you do not know. Examiners are looking for evidence that you have the relevant knowledge and that you under- stand the subject you have studied. You are *not* being examined on your memory as such, or on your ability to write at length. Of course, being able to remember is impor- tant, but not if you do not understand what you remember. If this sounds ridiculous, it is not. Think of a parrot which can automatically repeat 'Pretty Polly' or think of a rhyme such as 'Goosey, goosey gander'. Maybe you can say it but what does it mean? (It is *not* about geese.)

Examiners do not expect perfect answers. They do expect (or rather, hope for) coherent structured, legible *answers* to the questions set. Please note, you are expected to *answer the questions that have been asked*, not to 'Write all you know' about something or to regurgitate an essay you have previously written, which will probably *not* answer the question.

Do not, as some candidates do, answer a question they wish they had been set instead of the one that has. You will not be given credit for showing knowledge you have not been asked for. It is so sad when a candidate does this.

Examiners cannot mark a paper that does not indicate which questions have been answered. They cannot guess that you have answered Question 4 unless you tell them so. Examiners will be thoroughly irritated by papers which are muddled and confused, with papers out of order and unclear. How will they know that the continuation of your essay is somewhere in the muddle?

When marking hundreds, sometimes thousands, of anonymous scripts, no examiner is going to spend time searching for the next part of a question if you have not numbered or referenced it clearly. It is exasperating, to say the least, to read what is clearly a good answer but not to know what it is! It is not part of an examiner's job to sort your work out. That is your responsibility. Neither will an examiner be aware that you did not wish these rough notes to be marked if you have not crossed them out. It may even appear to him or her that you have answered the same question twice! Unfortunately there will still only be one set of marks for the question. The 'first' will be marked and the second ignored.

At an advanced level, examiners comment on student failure to be aware of the verb in essay instructions. Also, they remark on the lack of logical arguments (which leads to unacceptable conclusions) on general, anecdotal, answers, or essays full of personal value judgments, based on banal opinions rather than knowledge.

Do remember that you are usually anonymous to the examiners. They do not know who you are. Your tutor or teacher will know what you can do, an 'outside' examiner will not know. Even then, your teacher or tutor will be unable to help you if you do something silly. It is not you who is being examined; it is your work.

Be courteous to the examiner. Make your work easy to read. Difficult, certainly when under pressure and working to time, but do try. Obey the instructions on the paper and answer the questions you are asked. Number your choices and papers too if necessary. Ensure that all parts of your paper can be identified as yours. Hand in a coherent, well-worked script. That is what examiners want.

Some possible 'pitfalls' or 'sillies'

There are several ways in which even good students can fail to do as well as they could have done in an examination. Very often, candidates can make silly mistakes which could have been easily avoided, much to examiners' despair. The following are examples of some common 'sillies':

1. Failure to read the instructions properly which leads to:
    (a) answering too many questions,
    (b) answering an insufficient number of questions,
    (c) not recognising compulsory questions,
    (d) not recognising either/or questions,
    (e) not recognising instructions about multi-part questions.
2. Being unaware of mark distribution which leads to:
    (a) long answers for few possible marks, so wasted time,
    (b) short answers for more possible marks, therefore very few marks for the question,
    (c) unbalanced time division, therefore loss of possible marks.
3. Not numbering answered questions clearly.
4. Not crossing out rough work after the answer has been written.

5.   Rewriting an answer or changing one's mind and doing another question, *but leaving them both in!*

6.   Running out of time and not completing the paper. If only three out of four possible questions are answered, this means an immediate loss of 25% of the total marks available, making the only possible *total* mark of 75%. Even if a candidate has spent ages on a wonderful answer to one of the three completed questions, it still will not carry him to 80%.

7.   Rushing into the paper without careful thought and using wrong formulae throughout. Panic?

8.   Misreading signs (plus, minus, divide). Rushing? Panic?

9.   Misreading a vital word in the question, e.g. 'macro' for 'micro'.

10. Misspelling a vital explanatory word, e.g. 'allusion' – 'illusion', 'causal' – 'casual'.

11. Deciding you do not like what you have done and crossing it out BEFORE rewriting. Then the bell rings, 'Pens down, please. Stop writing'.

If you are allocated 2½ hours to complete a paper, for example, you are not likely to do very well if you try to do the paper twice in that time. Anyway, you should not be in that situation if you have worked well beforehand. If you have prepared and planned in the controlled manner that this chapter advises, the more you feel in control, the more you will be able to control any nervousness or anxiety.

Note this example of a 'silly'. A group of 'A' level students, intelligent and hardworking, had spent one afternoon a week, for the previous few weeks, doing practice examinations under the eagle eye of their teacher. The teacher had tried, by analysing previous papers over past years, to set questions which she felt might be asked in the examinations that year. Much to the teacher's delight, the analysis worked. Several of the topics did turn up in the paper. At least two of them in almost the same form as had been already seen, worked and discussed by her students. However, not *one* student recognised any of this. Why? Nervousness and anxiety can cause 'sillies'.

Pre-examination preparation
The solid work has been done, examination day is almost here. You have dealt with much of the 'unknown' by now. You know what the paper or papers will look like and how long you will be given to answer the questions. You will know how many questions you must answer and how the marks will be distributed. Even if the format of the paper changes a little you are still prepared for that as you are aware of the possibility. You have done what you expect to do many times.

Venue – where?
Familiarise yourself with this. If you have to travel to the place where you will be examined, make your travel plans ahead of time. How will you get there? How long will it take you? Visit beforehand if the venue is strange to you. Get the 'feel' of the place. Find your way around. Where are the cloakrooms? Is there a cafeteria? Where are the lifts or stairs? Where are the notice boards which will tell you where you have to be and when? Reception? Parking? Which entrance? You do not want to be rushing about finding these things out on the day.

Make absolutely sure that you have the day, date and time correct. Check and check again. Write it all down if you have not been given an official notification. Write it all down anyway. It is comforting to *do* something practical.

Challenge

Yes, of course you will be nervous. It would be more worrying if you were not. No one can expect to sit an examination without feeling some stress. Anxiety levels for individuals are not the same but do bear in mind that some of your fellow students would never admit to 'nerves' whilst others 'run around in small circles' not caring who sees them. Neither attitude is ideal. Too much stress is debilitating, tantamount to illness; too little, or none, is unrealistic and could be a sign of misplaced confidence. We need a mixture of determination, anxiety *and* confidence that comes from knowing that we have done our best so far and that we will, because of that, do our best in the examination. A certain amount of stress is needed to stimulate the mind and body to take on a challenge. Will our best be good enough? We will not know until we try. Remember that many thousands of students have taken this examination before you, many thousands no doubt will take it in the future. The majority survive!

Think of your course as a journey and the examination as the terminus; the end of the journey; your goal. Any stops on the way (objectives), take you nearer to your journey's end. You have packed your bags, you have all you need (knowledge, learning, understanding). All you need now is your ticket to go through the barrier at the terminus. You are prepared; that is your ticket.

How you spend the short time before the examination is up to you. By now, you know your own needs best. Some students prefer to relax completely, to take time off from study and temporarily 'forget' their anxiety. Others prefer to deal with pre-examination feelings by continuing to revise until the last moment. You will need to eat properly and sleep properly, or as well as you can. You must give your mind and body the chance to move into top gear when you ask them to. A drugged sleep and an empty inside is *not* advised.

On examination day itself, there are several things you can do to make yourself feel physically more in control. Controlled breathing will help you. Do not breathe too deeply and make yourself dizzy though! Calm your breathing down, do not rush, try to relax the tension in your body as much as you can. Relaxation techniques are taken seriously today and can be of great benefit to anyone who finds himself becoming particularly tense and nervous under stress. Investigate the possibility of learning such techniques beforehand if you feel they may benefit you.

Immediate preparation

Be practical. Having found out what will be needed and/or allowed in the examination room, collect all these things together the night before the examination. Prepare your watch, pens, pencils, sharpener, rulers, calculators, mathematical instruments, rubbers, dictionaries (if allowed), texts (if allowed), and add extras in case something fails to work.

Then look after yourself. Take tissues, sweeties (if allowed) and check spectacles if you wear them. Prepare your clothes for the next day, taking the venue into account. Big glass windows for example can make a room into a 'greenhouse' or 'hot house'. A large room with little heating can be very cold in winter. Be comfortable. Be sure to have comfortable feet! You do not want to be distracted by a painful toe! If you think the room may be hot, wear layered clothing so that you can remove a layer with decency. Layered clothing is a good idea anyway. Think how much harder it would be to concentrate on your answers if you were dreadfully hot in thick irremovable clothes (with sore feet!), *and* a headache, because you had forgotten your glasses. Students <u>have</u> been known to faint.

144 The Exam Secret

Examination Day

Be on time. Not too early. You do not want to wait too long before you are allowed to enter the examination room. Not too late – it will not be good for your stress levels to arrive breathless and find you have to clatter into a silent examination room before a lot of disapproving stares. After a certain time you would not be allowed to enter anyway – there goes your chance, marked 'absent'.

Permission to enter? Take your seat. Your examination number will be (or should be) on the desk which has been allocated to you. There should be a clock ahead of you, or somewhere where it can easily be seen. Synchronise your watch with that. Sometimes the clock is put on the wall by an invigilator as the examination begins. Synchronise at the start, then you can keep your head down most of the time, just using the clock for a quick time check occasionally.

Put all you need on your desk. Make sure you leave nothing in your bag that you might need later. Your bag will probably be removed if you have not had to leave it at the door already. Make sure your tissues are handy – very useful for propping up a wobbly desk, if nothing else. They are better than writing paper as they are more squashy! Little things help at this stage.

Ready for the challenge?

You may find paper on the desk already and even sometimes the examination paper, turned over so that you cannot see the questions yet. Leave it alone! If the paper is not there, the invigilator will give them out before the examination begins. You will have been asked by now to be completely silent. From now on, any form of contact with another candidate will automatically be suspect. Even if all you wish to do is to make eye contact or an innocent remark, do *not* do so. Neither must you acknowledge a remark by another candidate. All queries from now on must be directed at the invigilator. Ignore all else around you. Pay attention only to the invigilator. If you have a problem, put your hand up. Do nothing at all whilst waiting to begin, unless you are allowed to put your name on the paper.

Then, when you are told, 'You may begin'.

First
Read the instructions, ever so carefully. But you know that by now. Then, having read and understood the instructions, scan the paper. Quickly, but carefully.

See how it is arranged. If you have choices, mark the questions you feel you could do.

Read these questions again. Choose. Mark your choices. You may wish to mark them in an order of 1, 2, 3 etc., in which you will do them. You may wish to begin with the choice which is first on the paper and carry on to the next. Whatever you do, do not dither.

Then, check your timing. You will have practised organising time allocation whilst doing practice papers. This will stand you in good stead now. Divide your time into the number of *equal mark* questions you have to answer. Equal marks, equal time. Note the time by which you need to begin and complete each answer on the paper. Write the times by each question. Remember planning and checking time. You have already used reading time, so take that off.

Time out of your allocation spent making a brief plan of your intended answer is time well spent. It will prevent you meandering away from the point as you write. You will have a structure to work from, to support your answer.

Before you plan, you must analyse your questions. Note what you must do: 'account for', 'consider' and so on, if the answer is in essay form. If it is, then you will know by now what form of title analysis suits you best. You must be quick though. Do not dawdle.

Write the question number and begin. Make yourself start, however you feel. Write something. When you have completed that answer, do the next one and then the next one, until you have answered all the questions required. Check your timing throughout so that you can speed up the completion of an answer if necessary, so as to move on. Try not to 'run over' the time you have set yourself. If you do, be aware that you now have less time for the other questions.

Put your hand up for more paper well *before* you need it to continue. You do not want to be sitting, waiting, wasting precious time, whilst the invigilator sees to someone else. Hand up, continue writing. Do not look up. Carry on.

Some students feel more in control if they plan each answer first before beginning the answers themselves. This means that timing will need adjustment. Practice beforehand will show which approach is best for you. Bear in mind that you will have to change topic concentration more often. Do not confuse the brief plan you need to make with the short draft that you have been making during coursework. There is no time for this now. Use the plan to guide you to the paragraphing and structure of your final answer.

Do try to leave yourself some time to check your work. Check spellings, vocabulary, grammar and punctuation. You can often gain marks here as we have seen. Check what you have said. Check any formulae and processes used for correctness. Most importantly, check question numbers and paper numbers. Check again, that you have done what the instructions have told you to do. No more, no less.

Cross out any work that you do not want the examiner to mark. Do not cross work out until it has been used or replaced though. If you run short of time, use what little time remains to make the brief notes that you would have used to answer the final question; even if you cannot complete the answer itself, jot the remaining points down quickly. Do *not* cross these out. You will gain some credit for what you say as it can show the examiner that you know what you are talking about.

Similarly, in mathematics or science, if you can show that you understand the processes by showing correct workings and methodology, you will be credited with some marks even if you have done a 'silly'.

As the examination draws to an end, as the hands creep around the clock, you are still checking, correcting if need be, ensuring all loose papers are safely joined together, still totally absorbed in what you are doing. At least, you should be. Hopefully, you will not have been one of those unhappy people who left the room earlier, as soon as it was allowed, for whatever reason. This always happens to someone. It should not be you. Were they over confident and therefore unprepared? Perhaps. Nothing to do with you though.

You will be told to 'Stop writing now please' and you must do so. The only possible thing you could still be doing is numbering your pages or tying pages together, or at least something which has nothing to do with writing an answer. You have had your allocated time. Do not speak. You must remain silent until you are out of the room.

Your work may be collected from you before you are allowed to leave, or you may leave your work on the desk and go.

After the examination, no post-mortems please. Worrying about what you have or have not done, after you have or have not done it, does no good at all. There is nothing you can do about it now, the next paper is ahead of you. The next challenge. You need to prepare yourself for that. Hopefully, you will have learned so much from your first examination experience that you will be feeling positive about the challenge ahead. Note, 'positive', not overconfident.

Pay no heed to fellow students who may be complaining

or pessimistic. They are not you: you know what you have done and you *know* you have done your best.

Relax a little and unwind before you begin to revise again. If this is your final examination, just relax and unwind!

To sum up

1. Familiarise yourself with as many 'unknown' aspects of the examination as you can.
2. Make a revision timetable.
3. Condense your notes as you revise. Simplify your retrieval system if possible or necessary.
4. Rehearse – complete past papers. Develop timing techniques.
5. Examine as many past papers as possible to become familiar with the format.
6. Practise dealing with instructions.
7. Rehearse practical work as much as you can – to time.
8. Understand what examiners want.
9. Learn how to give examiners what they want.
10. Be aware of possible pitfalls.
11. Be practical (1) about place, (2) about time, (3) about yourself and what you will or might need.
12. Be in control, you have had many rehearsals.
13. Keep working until told to stop.
14. Check what you have done.
15. Forget it!

12

INTERNATIONAL ENGLISH LANGUAGE TESTING SYSTEM

It may be that some of the readers of this book will need, at some time, to apply from abroad to Colleges or Universities in the United Kingdom in order to further their studies. If this applies to you, you will find that the institution of your choice will probably require you to take an examination or 'test' to assess your competence in English.

Such a test will assess whether your command of the English language is sufficient for you to study or train using that language as a medium. It is a very useful test because it will show you how well, or otherwise, you should be able to cope with your chosen course.

The International English Language Testing System (IELTS) is a universally respected and recognised assessment procedure. You do not have to be in the United Kingdom to take the tests as there are many places throughout the world where you can do so. Details of these will be given to you if you write to one of the two addresses given at the end of this chapter.

British Council offices in most countries can provide you or your teachers or tutors with the information you might need. Tests can be arranged world-wide to meet demand at various suitable times and places. In the UK, tests are time-tabled at frequent intervals at different places throughout the year. Students should check available dates with centres convenient for them.

It is possible to send for practice test material for you to test yourself initially, to see whether it is worthwhile at that point to take a test and to see whether you are at the level required for what you wish to do. If not, then you know what you need to do to reach that level and you can work towards it.

About the tests

There are two levels of tests. One, the **Academic**, is for those of you who wish to study at under-graduate or post-graduate level at a university. The other, the **General Training** level, is for those who wish to further their education at secondary level or college. The tests are intended to assess different needs appropriately.

Both tests comprise four components, reading, writing, listening and speaking. The two last, listening and speaking, are common to both. There is a difference between the expectations of **Academic** and **General Training** reading and writing tests.

Listening 'module'

This is not subject based and applies to both levels of assessment. The test deals with topics of general interest which are considered to be accessible to everyone. Candidates listen to taped information and conversations and are expected to write answers to questions set on what they have heard. The questions vary in kind and become progressively more difficult. Expected reading is minimal.

Speaking 'module'

As with listening, this module is common to both levels. The candidate is expected to talk to a (friendly!) examiner about a topic which is of interest to him (the candidate), and also about himself and his intended studies. Candidates may also be expected to respond orally to information provided by the examiner.

Reading 'module'

Academic reading involves responding in writing to non-specialist, general interest texts of appropriate under-graduate or post-graduate level. There should be more than one text, one of which may be non-verbal; that is, it may present you with information in diagram, map or chart form. Another text may expect you to show the ability to follow logical argument and recognise the need to evaluate. Questions set will vary in kind as before, becoming more difficult as you progress.

The reading test for General Training will be looking for a less academic level of language use and understanding. It will provide a student with the opportunity to demonstrate his ability beyond a basic level. As before, there will be more than one test of increasing difficulty to assess the level of competence. Also as before, questions will vary in type.

Writing 'module'

The Academic writing test asks candidates to respond in more than one way to set tasks. As the earlier chapters on written work advise, students need to be aware of the *purpose* of the writing they are asked to do. One task might be concerned with a practical approach related to the interpretation of data or an explanation of diagrammatic information of some kind. Another task might ask for a more conventional, essay type format in which a candidate could be asked to 'evaluate', 'contrast' and 'compare', 'consider evidence' and so on.

Students who take the General Training writing test may be asked to do written work which includes letter writing or report writing of some kind. This could involve giving information, expressing an opinion or ideas, asking for information, or something similar. Candidates could also be asked a question or questions about a presented problem or point of view.

Whatever the level, the tests are intended to provide candidates with a realistic assessment of their ability to study at a particular level using the medium of the English language.

A final word. Those of you who may have sight or hearing disabilities should not be discouraged from considering the tests. Centres *do* make arrangements to cater for students who may have special needs. The student, or his teacher or tutor, should inform the centre if that is the case so that appropriate arrangements can be made.

For information about the IELTS Tests, apply to:

Subject Manager (IELTS)
University of Cambridge
Local Examination Syndicate
Syndicate Buildings
1 Hills Road
Cambridge
CB1 2EU
United Kingdom

Tel: +44 (0) 1223 553311
Fax: +44 (0) 1223 460278
E-Mail: guymer.l@ucles.org.uk

The British Council
(IELTS Enquiries)
58 Whitworth Street
Manchester
M1 6BB
United Kingdom

Tel: +44 (0) 161 957 7755
Fax: +44 (0) 161 957 7762
E-Mail: general.enquiries@britcoun.org

The Manager
IDP Education Australia
G.P.O. Box 2006
Canberra
ACT 2501
Australia

Tel: +61 2 6285 8222
Fax: +61 2 6285 3233
E-Mail: ielts@idp.edu.au

IELTS on the Internet:
http://www.ielts.org

CONCLUSION

If you have read, browsed, skimmed or scanned through this book and have found it of use, then it will have served its purpose.

You have been advised throughout to 'argue' with an author to involve yourself in your studies so that they are 'yours'. Do that also with this book. If you do, it means that you have developed the ability and confidence that the author wished to help you find.

If techniques suggested lead you to others *not* suggested, but which work for you, then that is good. That is what you need to do.

Many, many times, students have handed in work saying, 'Here is your work Miss'. No thank you. 'Your work, I think!'

INDEX

RIGHT WAY
PUBLISHING POLICY

HOW WE SELECT TITLES

RIGHT WAY consider carefully every deserving manuscript. Where an author is an authority on his subject but an inexperienced writer, we provide first-class editorial help. The standards we set make sure that every **RIGHT WAY** book is practical, easy to understand, concise, informative and delightful to read. Our specialist artists are skilled at creating simple illustrations which augment the text wherever necessary.

CONSISTENT QUALITY

At every reprint our books are updated where appropriate, giving our authors the opportunity to include new information.

FAST DELIVERY

We sell **RIGHT WAY** books to the best bookshops throughout the world. It may be that your bookseller has run out of stock of a particular title. If so, he can order more from us at any time – we have a fine reputation for "same day" despatch, and we supply any order, however small (even a single copy), to any bookseller who has an account with us. We prefer you to buy from your bookseller, as this reminds him of the strong underlying public demand for **RIGHT WAY** books. Readers who live in remote places, or who are housebound, or whose local bookseller is unco-operative, can order direct from us by post, by phone with a credit card, or through our web site.

FREE

If you would like an up-to-date list of all **RIGHT WAY** titles currently available, send a stamped self-addressed envelope to ELLIOT RIGHT WAY BOOKS, BRIGHTON ROAD, LOWER KINGSWOOD, TADWORTH, SURREY, KT20 6TD,U.K.
or visit our web site at www.right-way.co.uk